UNCLE DON'S ADVENTURE DOWN EAST

COOKBOOK

DONALD B. DREW

Donald B. Drew / Publisher / P.O. Box 251,
Cumberland Center, Maine 04021

Copyright © 1987 Donald B. Drew
All Rights Reserved
Printed in The United States of America

Donald B. Drew / Publisher / P.O. Box 251,
Cumberland Center, Maine 04021

I would like to express my sincere appreciation
to the following friends who have contributed to the
compilation of Uncle Don's Adventure Down East
Cookbook:
Don Crandall and Landmark School's Graphic
    Arts students
Barbara W. Leighton—Typing and Editing
Al Edwards—Art Work

Dedicated
to
My Friends for whom I cooked
at
LANDMARK SCHOOL
NORTH YARMOUTH ACADEMY
CAMP WIGWAM
&
UNCLE DON DREW'S WESTCUSTOGO INN
(Sept. 11 - June 30, 1985-1986)

A TRIBUTE

It is indeed a pleasure for me to be able to play a very small part in the preparation of this project for my good friend, Donald Drew.

It was in 1963, while I was employed at North Yarmouth Academy in Yarmouth, Maine as Secretary to the Headmaster, that I first met Don Drew. He came to the Academy fresh from Southern Maine Vocational Technical Institute in South Portland to assume the position of Chef for the dormitory population and staff at NYA. It was soon obvious that Don had chosen his profession wisely; he had a flair with food and knowing how to get along with people, young and old. In fact, it was these dormitory students who gave him the nickname "Uncle Don."

Over the years Don endeared himself to the school community. His kitchen was a bright spot on campus. A good disposition and a keen sense of humor were integral parts of his personality, and I can vouch for his credentials as a cook from personal experience and enjoyment of the meals he provided.

I want Uncle Don to know how much I have enjoyed our friendship and association over the years, and to wish the best of everything for him in future endeavors. Especially do I wish to thank him for the opportunity of sharing in this tremendous undertaking, the results of which may be, in turn, shared and enjoyed by so many other folks far and wide.

A friend,
Barbara W. Leighton

This is a Character Sketch by Al Edwards, made and presented to me in 1972 by my Friends at Landmark School in Prides Crossing when I was Director of Food Services from 1971 - 1985.

This was created from a photo taken at a buffet at North Yarmouth Academy, Yarmouth, Maine.

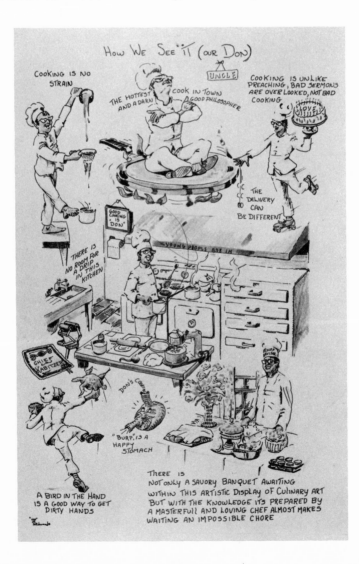

TABLE OF CONTENTS

Tribute 4
Preface. 8
Introduction 9
Weights & Measures. 11
Hors D'Oeuvres. 16
Soups. 26
Fish & Shellfish. 36
Salads & Dressings. 50
Raised Breads & Rolls. 64
Main Dishes. 78
Vegetables 98
Sauces for Vegetables & Meats. 112
Pastries. 118
Desserts & Puddings. 141
Cakes 152
Cookies 170
Frostings & Dessert Sauces. 184
Quick Breads. 194
Eggs. 206
Beverages 212
Cooking Tips

PREFACE

As books sold out on "An Adventure into Foodland with Uncle Don" and "Uncle Don's Down East Cookbook," I had many requests for more books and some new recipes.

This book includes all of the old Favorite recipes from my original books, plus some new recipes for your pleasure.

I hope that I have produced a compilation of recipes that will make this book a Favorite household item which will provide you with much pleasure.

"If it's good, don't Change it!"

You will notice that I have designed this book without an Index. However, the Table of Contents lists Sections with page numbers, and each Division page lists every recipe in that Section.

I have chosen this arrangement because so many times when you want to make something, you go right to that page and never look at anything else in the book. Don't waste a good book—read it from cover to cover and maybe a recipe will catch your eye and tickle the palate, and you have a new goodie to take to the meeting or to serve your guests.

I enjoy cooking for people who enjoy eating. Everyone has different tastes to please, so no one is happy all the time.

Experiment a little and create and bring out your own personality in the food and, on top of it all, put Love into your work.

Uncle Don

"Keep it plain and simple"

INTRODUCTION

The results of each recipe can vary a bit depending on different size eggs, flour used, and care given.

I do not sift any flour unless specifically mentioned in a recipe. Use flour just as it comes to you from the market.

I use medium size eggs, so if large or extra large eggs are being used, you may want to cut down a little, but only in recipes calling for more than 4 eggs, in which case you could cut 1 egg.

To make 1 cup of sour milk, I add 2 tbs. cider vinegar to 3/4 cup sweet milk and fill cup with milk.

I find that water used in pancakes, breads, and biscuits produces a more spongy texture than milk, but if you want the richness, you can use milk.

Creaming the shortening and sugar is mixing with wooden spoon or electric mixer until light and fluffy.

Before beginning to create a masterpiece you should follow these few simple rules:

1. Read the recipe to be sure you have everything you need.

2. Gather ingredients and have them ready.

3. Round up utensils: bowls, spoons, mixer, spatulas, pans, etc.

4. Set oven to proper temperature so that it will be hot when you are ready.

5. Measure ingredients carefully and as accurately as possible.

6. Pack brown sugar firmly in measuring container.

7. Measure flour without packing.

8. Follow directions on each individual recipe.

METRIC CONVERSION CHART

1 tsp.	=	4.9 cc
1 tbs.	=	14.7 cc
1/3 cup	=	28.9 cc
1/8 cup	=	29.5 cc
1/4 cup	=	59.1 cc
1/2 cup	=	118.3 cc
3/4 cup	=	177.5 cc
1 cup	=	236.7 cc
1 fl. oz.	=	29.5 cc
4 oz.	=	118.3 cc
8 oz.	=	236.7 cc
1 pt.	=	473.4 cc
1 qt.	=	.946 Liters
1 gal.	=	3.7 Liters

Liters	x	1.056	=	Liquid quarts
Quarts	x	.946	=	Liters
Liters	x	.264	=	Gallons
Gallons	x	3.785	=	Liters
Ounces	x	28.349	=	Grams
Grams	x	.035	=	Ounces
Pounds	x	.454	=	Kilograms
Kilograms	x	2.205	=	Pounds

TABLE OF WEIGHTS AND MEASURES

2 teaspoons	=	1 dessert spoon
3 teaspoons	=	1 tablespoon
4 tablespoons	=	1/4 cup
8 tablespoons	=	1/2 cup
16 tablespoons	=	1 cup
2 cups	=	1 pint
4 cups	=	1 quart
4 quarts	=	1 gallon
8 quarts	=	1 peck
Pinch-Dash	=	less than 1/8 teaspoon
Stream	=	2 teaspoons +

2 cups liquid	=	1 pound
2 cups butter or shortening	=	1 pound
2 cups granulated sugar	=	1 pound
3 3/4 - 4 cups flour	=	1 pound
1/4 pound butter	=	1/2 cup
1 7/8 cups rice	=	1 pound
2 cups chopped meat	=	1 pound
1 medium egg	=	2 ounces
2 2/3 cups powdered sugar	=	1 pound
2 2/3 cups brown sugar	=	1 pound

YOU CAN'T RUSH GOOD FOOD!!

SUBSTITUTIONS

1 square chocolate = 3 tablespoons cocoa + 1 1/2 tsp. shortening

1 tablespoon cornstarch = 2 tablespoons flour (as thickening)

1 teaspoon baking powder = 1/4 teaspoon baking soda + 1/2 tsp. cream of tartar

1 cup fresh milk = 1/2 cup evaporated milk + 1/2 cup water

1 cup sour milk = 2 tablespoons vinegar + 3/4 cup sweet milk (Fill cup with milk)

1 yeast cake = 1 pkg. dry yeast

Teaspoon	= tsp.
Tablespoon	= tbs.
Cup	= c
Minutes	= min.
Pound	= lb.

NOTES

NO WAITING!

HORS D'OEUVRES

Bacon-Franks

Cheese Puffs

Crab or Tuna Thins

Little Puffs

Olive Cheese Balls

Pick-a-Bobs

Shrimp Scampi

Stuffed Celery

Stuffed Eggs

Stuffed Mushroom Caps

Hot Broccoli Dip

Hot Crab and Shrimp Dip

Crabmeat Pizza Dip

Maine Clam Dip

BACON-FRANKS

Cut franks into 1 inch pieces. Wrap with strip of American cheese and raw bacon on outside, with toothpick through it. Broil until bacon is golden, about 5-8 min.

CHEESE PUFFS

Bring to boil (4 tablespoons butter
              (1 cup water

Add and cook (1/2 cup flour
  3-4 min.   (1/2 tsp. Worcestershire Sauce
            (1/2 cup grated Parmesan
             cheese

Remove and add 2 eggs

Beat mixture until smooth. Make balls the size of a nickel and bake at 350° for 25 min., or until a little dry. Serve warm. Makes about 5 dozen.

BROILED CRAB OR TUNA THINS

Make a mixture of flaked tuna or crabmeat with cream cheese until it spreads. Add chopped olives to taste. Spread on rye thins or cut squares of bread and bake in 400° oven for 8-10 min. or until golden brown.

LITTLE PUFFS

Make cream puff mixture from dessert section, but drop in balls the size of a quarter and bake at 400° for 20 min., or golden brown and firm.
Cut off tops and fill with:
Crabmeat with a little mayonnaise
Chicken diced, mayonnaise, salt and
pepper
Egg salad
Chopped ham with minced dill or sour
pickle

OLIVE-CHEESE BALLS

1 cup grated sharp cheese
3 tbs. soft butter
1/2 cup flour   24 olives
1/4 tsp. salt

Work ingredients together with fork or fingers until well blended. Wrap 1 tsp. dough around each olive. Refrigerate or freeze and bake at 400° for 10-15 min.

PICK-a-BOBS

Take small 1/2 inch cubes of raw steak or lamb and place on end of round wooden toothpick. Add small cherry tomato, or cut tomatoes, not too ripe, into small pieces. Add cube of raw onion, green pepper. Brush with melted butter with dash of garlic, salt and pepper, and broil for 5 min. or less.

SHRIMP SCAMPI

```
       ( 1 tbs. minced garlic
       ( 1 tbs. minced onion
Saute  ( 2 tbs. minced parsley
       ( 1/2 tsp. lemon
       ( 1/2 cup butter ( part olive oil )
       ( Dash of salt and pepper
```

Add 2 cups small raw shrimp and toss until cooked. Serve with toothpicks.

If preferred, place in ramekin and broil; turn and cook until golden brown.

STUFFED CELERY

Cut washed celery into 3-inch pieces and stuff with a mixture of:

1 package cream cheese
1 small pkg. roquefort cheese
Dash salt
Dash pepper
Dash worcestershire sauce

STUFFED EGGS

Hard boil 6 eggs; cool; cut lengthwise and place yolks in a bowl. Add to the yolks the following:

    3 tbs. softened butter
    1 tsp. worcestershire sauce
    1/2 tsp. salt
    Dash pepper
    Mayonnaise to make a soft mixture

Stuff above mixture back into the whites. Garnish with small sprigs of parsley, or dust lightly with paprika.

STUFFED MUSHROOM CAPS

Wash and remove stems. Dice stems and add a little crisp bacon bits or crumbled bacon. Mix in enough mayonnaise to make a paste, plus 2 tsp. parmesan cheese. Stuff caps and bake in 400° oven 8-10 min. on buttered cookie sheet.

HOT BROCCOLI DIP

1 pkg. Frozen chopped broccoli or 1 bunch of
   Fresh
2 tbs. butter
1 small onion diced
2 8-oz. pkg. cream cheese
1/4 tsp. Worcestershire Sauce
2 tbs. mayonnaise
1 tbs. Real lemon juice
Salt and pepper

Cook broccoli and set aside.

Saute onion in butter until golden brown. Add the
cooked and drained broccoli. Add rest of ingredients
and stir over low heat or in a double boiler until well
blended.

For a change sometime, add some chopped
mushrooms—1/2 cup to onions when browning.

Another time add 1/2 lb. sharp cheddar cheese
and melt in.

Also, they all go together.

HOT CRAB AND SHRIMP DIP

2 pkg. 8 oz. cream cheese
1 small can crabmeat or fresh crabmeat
1 small can shrimp or cooked fresh shrimp
1 tsp. Worcestershire Sauce
1/2 cup Chili Sauce
1 tbs. butter
Pepper to taste
2 drops Tabasco Sauce (optional)

Blend all ingredients in top of double boiler and serve in chafing dish or casserole dish with crackers or chips. May be heated in low temperature oven and held until ready to serve.

Make this also with lobster, or all or any combinations.

CRABMEAT PIZZA DIP

1 8-oz. pkg. cream cheese
2 tbs. mayonnaise
1 tsp. Worcestershire Sauce
1 tsp. lemon juice
1/2 bottle Chili Sauce
1 pkg. crabmeat, or 1 small can, drained

Mix cream cheese, mayonnaise, Worcestershire Sauce, and lemon juice, and spread on a round, flat plate. Spread Chili Sauce over, leaving a small border of white. Sprinkle with crabmeat, garnish with a little chopped parsley, and ready to dig into with Ritz or Triscuits or whatever.

MAINE CLAM DIP

1 can minced clams
1 8-oz. pkg. cream cheese
Dash of Worcestershire Sauce
Salt and Pepper
1 tbs. diced onion (optional)

Blend all ingredients together, reserving part of the clam juice until you know if you need all of it to make the thickness desired.

NOTES

"Ahh"

SOUPS

Clam Chowder

Fish Chowder

Lobster Stew or Crabmeat Stew

Corn Chowder

Cheese Soup

Minestrone

French Onion Soup

Cream of Tomato Soup

Cream of Mushroom Soup

Oyster Stew

Pea Soup

Soup Du' Leftovers

Cream of Carrot Soup

Cream of Broccoli Soup

Cream of Vegetable Soup

NEW ENGLAND CLAM CHOWDER (6-8)

4 medium size potatoes diced
1 medium onion diced
2 tbs. butter
1/4 cup diced salt pork or butter
2 cups water
2 cups milk (part cream or canned milk for a
                              richer chowder)
1 cup clams
Salt and pepper to taste

   (If desired, 1 can minced or chopped clams
   may be used in place of fresh clams)

   In heavy kettle brown salt pork and remove. If
using butter, just heat, add onions, and cook until
transparent. Add raw diced potatoes and cover with
water. Cook until tender.

   If using canned clams, use juice as part of the
2 cups of water. Add clams and simmer.

   Add milk which has been heated in separate pan.
Add salt, pepper, butter, and it is ready to eat.

   Place salt pork scraps on for garnish.

FISH CHOWDER

Make the same as Clam Chowder only add
1-2 lbs. of fresh haddock, cusk, or other white
fish when potatoes are still a little firm so that
the fish will cook and break up.

LOBSTER STEW (4-6)

2 chicken lobsters or a 1 1/2-2 lb. lobster
cooked. Saute meat in 4 tbs. butter; add dash
of paprika for color.

Add 4 cups hot milk and 1 small can of clam
bouillon for a little more flavor. (Part cream
or canned milk will make chowder richer)

Salt and pepper to taste and let set so that
the delicate lobster flavor will go through the
sweet milk and make a yummy stew.

Two 7 oz. packages of crabmeat may be
substituted for lobster for a nice crabmeat stew.

CORN CHOWDER (6-8)

Make the same as Clam Chowder except that instead of adding clams, add 1 can of cream style corn after potatoes have cooked.

During fresh corn season, left over cooked corn cut off cob makes a nice chowder, but use a little cream with milk to make it tastier.

CHEESE SOUP (8-12)

1/2 cup celery	Grind and then mea-
1/2 cup onions	sure. Cook together
1/2 cup carrots	in 3/4 cup butter un-
1/4 cup green peppers	til tender.

Add 1/2 cup flour and cook it in. Add 3 cups hot chicken stock or chicken bouillon. Add 2 cups grated sharp cheese. (May use some American) Stir until smooth.

Add 3 cups hot milk and 1/2 cup cream. Keep warm until served.

As with most soups, this one is better the next day.

MINESTRONE SOUP (6-8)

1 soup bone or around 8 bouillon cubes for 2 quarts of water.

1/2 cup cooked beans such as kidney, pea, or chick-peas. Soak dry beans over night and add to soup bone.

1 can tomatoes or 3 fresh ones cut into wedges
1/2 cup raw spaghetti or macaroni
1 cup shredded cabbage
3 chopped carrots
2 chopped medium onions
1 tbs. parsley

Cook soup bone, and beans if dry, until meat falls off, about 3 hours. If starting with beef bouillon, add all vegetables. (Others may be added according to what is in season or left in refrigerator.)

Simmer until vegetables are tender and then add 1/2 cup broken up spaghetti or elbow macaroni and cook another 20 min.

Serve with grated Parmesan cheese.

If bouillon is used, you may want to add diced meat.

FRENCH ONION SOUP (4-6)

3 medium size onions sliced in half moons
2 tbs. beef drippings or butter
6 cups boiling water with 6-7 bouillon cubes
Small stream of cooking sherry

Saute onions in fat until golden. Add water, bouillon, and sherry and simmer for 15 min. Serve with Parmesan cheese.

Croutons may be made by buttering slices of bread, sprinkling with Parmesan cheese, cutting to size desired, and browning in hot oven for a few minutes.

Use slices of homemade French bread for an extra treat.

FRESH CREAM OF TOMATO SOUP

1 small diced onion
1/4 cup butter + 2 tbs. flour
6 tomatoes washed and cut into 1/4's,
    peeled if heavy skinned
2 cups milk
1/2 cup cream

Cook onion in butter until transparent. Add tomatoes and simmer until cooked. Add 2 tbs. flour and cook in, then add hot milk. Simmer on low heat. Salt and pepper generously to taste.

To peel tomatoes, dip into boiling water for 10 seconds on a fork and then just peel skin back with knife. The same may be done by holding over an open flame on stove.

CREAM OF MUSHROOM SOUP

1/4 cup butter
2 tbs. flour
1 small diced onion
2 cups sliced mushrooms
2 1/2 cup milk, heated

Simmer onions and mushrooms in butter until tender, not too long. Add flour and stir in, then add hot milk, salt and pepper to taste, and simmer for a few minutes to cook the flour or it will taste pasty.

33

OYSTER STEW

2 cups milk
2 cups cream (half & half)
3 cups oysters (more or less)
1/3 cup clam juice (adds more flavor)
Salt and pepper
2 tbs. butter

Heat milk, cream, and clam juice in heavy pan or double boiler until it skims over. Add oysters and continue heating until the oysters start to curl. Add butter and ready to serve.

PEA SOUP

2 cups split peas
1 ham bone
2 qts. cold water
2 carrots
1 large onion
2 stalks celery
1/4 tsp. pepper

Soak peas in water overnight. Place ham bone in pot with cold water and all the vegetables except peas. Bring to a boil and then turn down and simmer for 1½ hours. Add peas, drained, and cook for another hour, or until peas are soft. Remove bone and rub the soup through a sieve, or if you like the coarseness, keep as is. Add pepper, and if you like a creamed pea soup, add some Half & Half to your base.

SOUP DU' LEFTOVERS

4 cups water
4 Bouillon cubes (beef or chicken)
3 small onions, diced
2 tbs. butter
2 cups any left over vegetables, meats, etc., or 2
    cups Frozen vegetables of your choice.
Salt and Pepper

Melt butter and saute onions until golden brown.
Add water and bouillon cubes and bring to a boil.
Add everything else and simmer on low heat until
ready to serve.

CREAM OF CARROT SOUP
CREAM OF BROCCOLI SOUP
CREAM OF VEGETABLE SOUP

1/4 cup butter
3 tbs. flour dissolved in 1/2 cup water
1 small onion diced
2 cups raw or frozen vegetables chopped
    or diced
2 cups milk heated
1 cup chicken stock (make with bouillon cube)
Salt and pepper to taste
Simmer onions and vegetables in butter until
onions turn translucent. Add chicken stock and simmer until vegetables are done to your taste, crispy or
well done. Add hot milk. Add flour and water and
cook until slightly thickened and flour taste has
cooked out. Serve with a sprinkle of parsley.
   For a rich soup, add a Sharp Cheddar Cheese
and let it melt into soup. Thickness of thinness can be
altered by adding or subtracting more flour and
water.

"Fresh"

SEAFOODS

Seafood Newburg

Lobster or Seafood Pie

Plain Old Boiled Lobster

Steamed Clams

Scalloped Clams or Scallops

Oven Baked Fish
  Haddock, Scrod, Sword, Sole

Baked Stuffed Fish

Shrimp Scampi

Fried Clams or Maine Shrimp

Salmon Wiggle — Tuna a la King

Sloppy Charlies

Tuna Noodle Casserole

Seafood Crumbs

Baked Haddock with Seafood Crumbs

Baked Stuffed Lobster

Creamed Finnan Haddie

Pan Fried Smelts

Baked Mackerel

Crabmeat Casserole

SEAFOOD NEWBURG

4 cups milk, heated
3/4 cup butter
3/4 cup flour

1/4 cup butter
1 small lobster (pick out meat)
1 pkg. crabmeat
1/2 lb. scallops
1/2 lb. shrimp cleaned and shelled

1/2 cup cooking sherry
Paprika

Heat milk in double boiler and set aside. Melt butter and add flour; cook for a few min. This is a roux.

Add roux to hot milk, a little at a time with a whisk so that it will not lump. Let this mixture cook on low heat in double boiler while you prepare the following:

Saute lobster and crab and paprika in 1/4 cup butter and add to cream sauce. Cover with water and bring to a boil the scallops and shrimp. Drain and put in cream sauce. Pour sherry in lobster pan and bring to a boil for 2 min. and add to cream sauce.

Hold on low heat for a while for better flavor, or make ahead and reheat on low heat in double boiler for more flavor.

LOBSTER OR SEAFOOD PIE

Make Newburg using only all one kind of fish. Place in baking dish and cover with flaky tender crust. Bake 30 min. or until golden brown and flaky.

PLAIN OLD BOILED LOBSTER
(The Favorite)

Take a kettle which will hold the number of lobsters you wish to cook. Place 2 - 3 inches of water in bottom, dash of salt, and bring to a boil. Place lobsters head first into boiling water and cover tight.

After it steams, it will take about 18 - 20 min. When the feeler snaps off easily, the lobsters are done. Over-cooking will make them tough.

Serve with melted butter.

Lobster is very delicate and should not be ruined by crazy recipes with over-powering spices. The plain and simple here is elegant.

STEAMED CLAMS

Wash well and, if sandy, place in water with a handful of corn meal for a couple of hours and then wash again. The corn meal cleans them.

Take a large kettle and pour about 1/2 inch water in bottom. Put in clams--a peck will serve about 4 people--and cover. Steam until clams just open, about 15 min. after they start to steam.

When eating, remove skin from neck, dip in bouillon, and then melted butter.

You are in for a feast!

Save some of your bouillon for making a stew, or for part of your liquid in Newburg.

SCALLOPED CLAMS   (4-6)

1 cup Ritz cracker crumbs
1 cup common cracker crumbs
1/2 cup melted butter
1 cup cream
1 cup milk
4 eggs
2 cups fresh whole clams, or chopped or
                                    canned clams
Dash salt and pepper

Mix cracker crumbs and butter together and alternate with clams in a buttered casserole dish, crumbs on bottom and ending with crumbs on top.

Beat eggs, milk, cream, salt and pepper. Pour over top and take a fork and poke a few holes so that mixture soaks through the rest. Bake in 375° oven 20-25 min. until it puffs and is golden brown.

The same may be done with diced scallops or shrimp.

OVEN BAKED FISH
(The only way)

Wash and place in a well buttered baking dish. Butter generously and squeeze a fresh lemon over top. Lots of lemon juice cuts oil in fish and takes out strong fish taste that children don't like.

Add salt and pepper. If you want, you may throw a few crumbs on top.

Bake in a 400° oven for 15-20 min., or until it flakes with a fork. A hot oven for a short time will give you moist, juicy fish every time.

I use this same method for haddock, sole, swordfish, and scrod.

BAKED STUFFED FISH

Choose your fish and prepare it the same as for oven baked.

1 cup common cracker crumbs
1 cup Ritz cracker crumbs
1/2 cup bread crumbs
1/2 cup melted butter
1 tsp. lemon juice
3 eggs
2 tbs. sherry
Dash of garlic powder (optional)
1 cup water

Mix everything together and place on top of fish. Liquid may vary as to whether you prefer a loose or a dry dressing on your fish.

Bake at 375° for about 30 min. or until fish flakes.

For shrimp, split and fill with stuffing, or use Maine shrimp in casserole with stuffing on top.

HOW SWEET IT IS!

FRIED CLAMS OR MAINE SHRIMP

Blend 1 3/4 cups milk, 4 eggs. Add and beat smooth:

    2 cups flour
    1 tsp. baking powder
    Dash of salt
    1 tbs. melted butter
    1 tsp. sugar
    Pinch of ginger (Prevents soaking)

Batter should be so that it just coats clam. If too thick they will be all batter; if too thin, it's nothing.

Fry in deep fat in an iron fry pan or deep pan at 375°. Turn both sides until golden brown. Drain on brown paper.

Cooked or raw shrimp can be done the same. Remove shells or they can be very crunchy!!!!

SALMON WIGGLE - TUNA a la KING

Cook together 2 tbs. butter, 2 tbs. flour, salt and pepper and add to 1 cup scalded milk with a whisk for a thin white sauce.

Add 1 can flaked salmon and 1/2 cup cooked frozen peas OR 1 can drained flaked tuna and a little pimento and peas for color.

Serve on buttered toast or hot fluffy tender biscuits.

SLOPPY CHARLIES

1 can drained tuna
1/2 can condensed mushroom soup
1 tbs. mayonnaise
1 tbs. diced raw onion
1 tbs. diced green pepper
1/2 tsp. Worcestershire sauce
Salt and pepper
Sliced cheese

Combine above and heap on an open hamburger bun. Top with a slice of cheese and bake in a 400° oven until cheese melts and is golden brown, 8-10 min.

TUNA NOODLE CASSEROLE

4 cups cooked macaroni
1 can cream of mushroom soup
1 large can flaked tuna
1 cup grated Chedder cheese
Salt and pepper
1/2 cup milk

Place mixture in buttered casserole dish. Cover with bread crumbs or cracker crumbs, dot with butter, and dust with paprika. Bake in 350° oven for 30 min.

SEAFOOD CRUMBS

2 cups crushed Ritz crackers
Small amounts of lobster, scallops, shrimp and
crabmeat diced all through the crumbs.

You may use as much or as little seafood as you want, or choose any one seafood. This is the same Crumbs I use to stuff Baked Stuffed Lobster.

Dribble melted butter over top.

Also good on Scallops or Shrimp.

BAKED HADDOCK WITH SEAFOOD CRUMBS

Place Haddock in a well buttered casserole dish, skin side down. Sprinkle lemon juice over fish generously. (Lemon juice cuts oil and takes out strong fish taste.)

Cover with Seafood Crumbs and drip melted butter over top. Bake in a 400° oven for 15 - 20 min. until fish flakes with a fork.

This was a Favorite at Uncle Don Drew's Westcustogo Inn.

BAKED STUFFED LOBSTER

Place lobster face down on cutting board. Use a sharp pointed knife. Push the point of the knife down through the head, between the eyes. This kills the lobster instantly. Turn over and cut whole length and spread apart. Remove head area and throw away. Save the tamale to mix into Crumbs.

Stuff the lobster with Seafood Crumbs and drizzle melted butter over top. Make slits in side of tail to keep from curling up.

Bake in hot oven 425° for around 20 min. If it starts to brown too much, place a leaf of lettuce or foil over Crumbs.

CREAMED FINNAN HADDIE

1# Finnan Haddie
1 diced small onion
1 recipe Cream Sauce
Ritz cracker crumbs
Melted butter

Place fish in a little water in a covered sauce pan. Simmer until it flakes—15 to 20 min.

Drain, remove any bones, and place in a buttered casserole dish. Saute onions until golden brown, add to Cream Sauce, and pour over fish. Sprinkle crushed Ritz crackers over top and drizzle butter over that.

Bake in hot oven 400° about 10 min., just to cook Crumbs, or place under broiler.

PAN FRIED SMELTS

Cut off heads and tails and slit down the middle. Clean out inside. Wash well in cold water.

Fry pork scraps, or bacon, or use melted butter in pan.

Roll smelts in corn meal or a little flour, salt and pepper.

Place in hot fat from above and gently turn until golden brown on both sides. These cook quickly, so do not over cook.

BAKED MACKEREL

Clean and split mackerel and place in a baking pan. Sprinkle salt and pepper and pour about 1/2 inch of milk in pan. Bake uncovered at 375° about 30 min., or until fish flakes. Bones can be lifted out easily if care is used. This is plain and simple and tasty.

The milk cuts the oily fish taste.

CRABMEAT CASSEROLE

1 tbs. butter
1 tbs. flour
1/2 cup milk (heated)
2 tsp. minced onions
1/2 tsp. Worcestershire Sauce
1/2 cup cubed white bread (not packed)
12 oz. to 1 lb. crabmeat
1/2 cup mayonnaise
1 tbs. lemon juice
1 egg beaten
Dash of salt, pepper, paprika

Melt butter and saute onions until translucent. Stir in flour and cook on low heat. Stir to keep from burning.

Add hot milk and bring to a boil, and cook until thickened. Add bread crumbs, Worcestershire Sauce, and crabmeat. Spoon into individual casseroles or a casserole dish.

Mix mayonnaise, lemon juice, egg, salt and pepper and spread over casserole. Sprinkle with paprika and bake at 450° for 10 min., or place under a low broiler until golden brown.

Serves 4 to 6 people

" ZIPPY TANGY DRESSING "

SALADS

Potato Salad
Cole Slaw
Bacon, Lettuce, and Tomato Salad
Tossed Salad
Tomato and Cucumber Salad
Spinach Salads
Fresh Fruit Salad
Three Bean Salad
Waldorf Salad
Macaroni Salad
Strawberry-Cranberry Salad
Removing gelatin salads from molds
Frosty Lime-Pineapple Salad
Summer Ambrosia
Tomato Aspic
Fresh Fruit Mold

SALAD DRESSINGS

Rich Red French

Sweet, Zippy, Tangy

999 Island

Caesar

Roquefort or Blu Cheese

Green Goddess

Fruit

POTATO SALAD (6-8)

1 medium onion
6 potatoes
2 hard boiled eggs
1 tbs. chopped parsley
4 tbs. vinegar
2 tbs. sugar
Dash ground cloves
Salt and pepper
Mayonnaise

Boil potatoes with skins on until tender. Peel while warm and cut into bowl.

Dice onion, cover with vinegar, sugar, and cloves and bring to a boil for 1 minute. Pour over potatoes, add salt and pepper, and enough mayonnaise to give good consistency. This will vary with size of potatoes. Add sliced hard boiled eggs and parsley.

By boiling the onions, they will never upset your stomach, and it removes the sharp onion taste from the salad.

This is a sweet-sour potato salad. If you prefer it plain, omit sugar and cloves.

COLE SLAW

Shred cabbage very thin, about 4 cups, and 2 carrots sliced or shredded. Add 1/4 cup vinegar, 1/2 cup mayonnaise, 2 tbs. sugar, salt and pepper. Toss and serve.

Another dressing would be 1/2 cup oil, 6 tbs. vinegar, 2 tbs. sugar, salt and pepper.

Some people like thin sliced green pepper in their Cole Slaw with the oil and vinegar dressing.

BACON, LETTUCE, AND TOMATO SALAD

Chop 1 head lettuce. Add 3 tomatoes cut in wedges, 8 slices of cooked crisp bacon broken into bits, 1/3 cup mayonnaise, more or less to taste, and salt and pepper.

TOSSED SALAD

You call it, lettuce is the most popular green, and is most always available. But for a change, you can always add romaine, Chinese cabbage, escarole, watercress, or chicory.

Always keep greens crisp, wash and pat dry with towel or paper towels, and keep refrigerated. Use your imagination.

Other ingredients you may use:

Tomato wedges	Red or white
Carrot curls or thin slices	onion rings
Cucumbers	Olives
Radishes	Avocado slices
Celery	Green peppers

FRESH TOMATO AND CUCUMBERS

Wash and cut 3 tomatoes in wedges. Peel and slice 2 cukes. For fresh garden cukes, wash and score with fork.

Pour Sweet and Sour dressing over them and serve.

SPINACH SALADS

Wash 1 bag fresh spinach and crisp. The following combinations will enhance it:

1. 4 sliced hard boiled eggs
    6 slices of crisp cooked bacon broken
        into bits, or "bacon bits canned"
    Sweet and tangy dressing

2. 1 can drained grapefruit and orange
        sections or 2 grapefruit and 2
        oranges sectioned
    Creamy fruit dressing

3. About 8-10 fresh mushrooms washed·
        and sliced thin
    Caesar dressing

FRESH FRUIT SALAD

Arrange sliced fresh fruits on a bed of lettuce and pour a little Creamy fruit dressing over them--

Cantaloupe balls or chunks
Watermelon "   "   "
Blueberries, whole
Strawberries, whole
Peaches
Apples sliced and coated with a little lemon
Bananas, the same as apples
OR
Canned fruits for salads and add fresh fruits in season to add a little sparkle.

THREE BEAN SALAD

1 can drained green beans
1 can drained wax beans
1 can drained Kidney beans packed in
            water
1 medium onion sliced thin

Cover with Sweet-zippy-tangy dressing
and get the best flavor after they have set
several hours. Make ahead and keep on hand.

WALDORF SALAD

Select 6-8 red crisp apples. Wash and
core and cut into cubes. The peelings add
nice color but you may peel them if you wish.

Add : 1 cup chopped celery
        1/2 cup chopped walnuts
        About 1/3 cup mayonnaise

For a little zip squeeze juice of 1/2 lemon
and add with a little grated rind.

MACARONI SALAD

1 cup elbow macaroni
1 green pepper diced
1 medium onion diced
1/2 cup diced celery
1 small can pimento diced
3/4 cup mayonnaise
2 tbs. vinegar
2 tbs. sugar
1/2 tsp. salt
1/2 tsp. pepper
1 tsp. prepared mustard

Cook macaroni until tender in salted boiling water. Drain, cool, and add all ingredients. Let set so that the flavor will go into the macaroni.

STRAWBERRY-CRANBERRY SALAD

2 cups fresh cranberries
1 pkg. raspberry gelatin
1 pkg. frozen strawberries
2 apples diced
1/2 cup chopped walnuts
1 cup water

Wash and drain cranberries. Bring to a boil in 1 cup water and cook until they pop open and darken in color. Remove from stove. Add 1 pkg. gelatin and dissolve. Add 1 pkg. frozen strawberries which will cool and thicken gelatin. Add apples and walnuts. Pour into mold and set.

REMOVING GELATIN SALADS FROM MOLDS

1. Have serving dish ready
2. Have pan large enough to set mold
      into to dip
3. Fill pan with hot water
4. Dip mold right to top for 5 seconds:
      lift and shake to loosen; invert
      and dump, still shaking
5. Garnish with parsley

Repeat if necessary

FROSTY LIME-PINEAPPLE SALAD

1 pkg. lime gelatin
1 cup boiling water
1 small can crushed pineapple
1/2 cup chopped celery
1 cup cottage cheese
1/4 cup mayonnaise
3 stiffly beaten egg whites

Dissolve gelatin in boiling water. Cool until it starts to thicken.

Add rest of ingredients except egg whites and stir until frosty colored.

Fold in beaten egg whites gently and pour into mold.

COOL SUMMER AMBROSIA

1 pkg. orange gelatin
1 cup boiling water
1 small can drained crushed pineapple
1 small can drained orange sections or
        3 oranges sectioned
1 cup miniature marshmallows
1/2 cup shredded coconut
3 egg whites beaten stiff

Follow directions as for Frosty Lime salad.

TOMATO ASPIC

1 1/2 cups tomato or V-8 juice
1/4 tsp. sugar
Pinch of cloves
1/2 tsp. Worcestershire sauce
1/2 tsp. salt
1/2 tsp. pepper
1 tbs. plain gelatin soaked in 1/4 cup
        cold water
1 tsp. lemon juice

Heat juice; dissolve gelatin mixture in hot juice. Add rest of ingredients and pour into mold or pan and cut into squares when firm.

FRESH FRUIT MOLD

1 pkg. raspberry gelatin
1 cup boiling water
1/2 cup whipped topping or cream
3 stiffly beaten egg whites

Dissolve gelatin in boiling water and cool until it starts to thicken. Add one of the following fruits or combinations. Fold in whipped topping and then gently fold in the egg whites.

Choices

2 cups diced fresh peaches
2 cups fresh strawberries sliced
2 cups fresh raspberries whole
2 cups sliced bananas
2 cups melon balls

This also makes a nice light dessert served with a little extra whipped cream.

RICH RED FRENCH DRESSING

1 cup oil
3/4 cup vinegar
1/2 cup sugar
1/2 cup catsup
1 tsp. salt
1 tsp. pepper
1/4 tsp. granulated garlic or
garlic salt
1/4 tsp. celery salt or seed

Blend well and serve.

SWEET ZIPPY TANGY DRESSING

1 cup oil
3/4 cup vinegar
1/2 cup sugar
1 tsp. salt
1 tsp. pepper
1/2 tsp. ground cloves
1/4 tsp. dry mustard

Blend well and serve.

999 ISLAND DRESSING

1 cup mayonnaise
1/4 cup chili sauce
1/4 cup catsup
1/4 cup drained green relish
1 tsp. salt
1 tsp. pepper
6 stuffed olives diced (optional)

Blend and serve.

CAESAR DRESSING

1 cup olive oil
1/2 cup lemon juice
2 crushed or diced garlic cloves
1 tsp. salt
1 tsp. pepper
2 eggs
1/2 cup parmesan cheese

Blend and serve.

For Caesar Salad, use fresh crisp romaine lettuce, anchovies, croutons, and a dribble of Caesar dressing.

ROQUEFORT OR BLU CHEESE DRESSING

Blend enough vinegar into 1/4 lb. of cheese to make a creamy paste. Add 1 tsp. salt, 1 tsp. pepper, 2 cups sour cream, 1/3 cup mayonnaise.

GREEN GODDESS DRESSING

1/2 cup mayonnaise
1/2 cup sour cream
3 tbs. vinegar
1 tbs. anchovy paste
2 tbs. chopped fine parsley
2 tbs. chopped fine chives,
    scallions, or onion
2 tsp. lemon juice
1/2 tsp. salt
1/2 tsp. pepper

FRUIT SALAD DRESSING

1/2 cup whipped cream or topping
1/4 cup mayonnaise
2 tbs. fruit juice (orange, cherry, or
    juice drained from canned fruit)
2 tsp. grated orange or lemon rind
                    (optional)

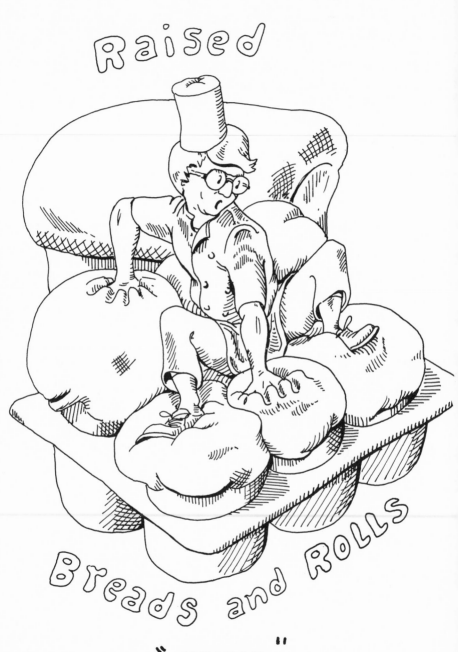

"**WHOA!!**"

RAISED BREADS AND ROLLS

White Bread

French Bread

Raisin Bread

Oatmeal Bread

Cornmeal Molasses Bread

Dark Rye Bread

Dinner Rolls

Butterhorn Rolls

Cloverleaf Rolls

Cinnamon Rolls

Christmas Stollen

RAISED BREADS AND ROLLS

Nothing is nicer than to walk into a kitchen and smell the aroma of homemade bread rising, and the joy that comes from fumes wafting through the air from moist, delicate, crusty hot yeast breads baking in the oven.

Yeast breads are easy to master if you take a few precautions:

1. Add yeast to lukewarm liquids--too hot will kill; too cold won't start.
2. Stir in all flour well.
3. Let rise in a warm place with no strong drafts.
4. Make sure oven is hot when bread goes in.

The best breads are made with flour high in gluten because cell structure is built better. But today's all-purpose flour makes a fine loaf of bread, and bread flour is not essential.

I always butter the tops of my bread after I shape the loaves. This makes a soft, golden brown, yummy crust.

WHITE BREAD

White bread is the standard loaf made most frequently, and varies very little in most cook books. This bread can be made into rolls, or have raisins or other dried fruits kneaded into it.

1 1/2 cups scalded milk, or just hot water
    for a bread not so rich
2 tbs. sugar
1 tbs. salt
2 tbs. shortening, either white or butter
2 pkg. dry yeast dissolved in 1/2 cup warm
    water
6 cups flour, plus a little more if dough is
    too sticky to the touch. Flours vary in the
    amount of liquid they can absorb.

Scald milk or use hot water. Add sugar, salt, and shortening. Let cool until lukewarm, then add yeast and water. Stir in one-half of the flour and then the rest.

Turn out on lightly floured surface and knead until smooth and elastic, about 5-8 min. Place in greased bowl, cover with a light cloth, and let rise until double in bulk, about 2 hours. If kitchen is cool, you may set it over a kettle of warm water, or turn on oven for just a few minutes, then off so that it isn't over 80° When you take dough out, be sure to preheat oven to 400° for baking.

Divide dough into two parts; knead and shape into loaves for greased pans; let rise covered for about 1 hour or doubled in bulk. Bake at 400° for 10 min., then turn to 350° for 40-50 min. until golden brown and comes loose from pan. For a soft crust I brush with shortening before loaves rise in pans.

FRENCH BREAD

2 cups hot water
4 tbs. shortening
1 1/2 tbs. salt
2 pkg. dry yeast
4 egg whites
9 cups flour

Place water in bowl; add shortening and salt; let cool to lukewarm. Add yeast and dissolve. Add 1 cup flour and mix in. Add egg whites and blend. Add rest of flour to make a very stiff dough. Follow directions for white bread only let rise, punch down, rise again, and then shape into 2 long loaves. Brush with another raw egg white which makes it crusty and shiny. Let rise and bake on baking sheet with cornmeal sprinkled on it. Bake in 400° oven 40-50 min. or until it sounds hollow when you tap it.

Note: Cut diagonal slashes in bread to let steam out. This keeps it from cracking all over as it expands.

This makes excellent garlic bread by slicing down and brushing with melted butter and garlic in it and wrapping in aluminum foil and heating in oven.

Also, slice, brush with garlic butter, and place under broiler for few minutes until golden buttery brown and you have garlic toast. Good for fondue or making croutons.

RAISIN BREAD

2 cups scalded milk
5 tbs. sugar
1 1/2 tbs. salt
3 tbs. shortening
2 pkg. dry yeast
1 egg, beaten
1/2 tsp. cinnamon
6 cups flour
3/4 cup raisins

Scald milk and add sugar, salt, cinnamon, and shortening. Cool to lukewarm and add yeast and beaten egg. Stir in 2 cups flour until smooth. Add raisins* and rest of flour. Knead, let rise, punch down, and let rise again—same as white bread only two rises. Butter pans and bread, let rise, and bake at 375°.

Go and do your dishes and clean the kitchen and your bread will be ready—about 1 hour.

*I boil my raisins for 5 min. in water and let set for 15 min. Drain and add to bread. This way they break up all through the bread and don't fall out as much when you slice it; also keeps the bread moist.

OATMEAL BREAD

2 cups hot water
1 cup oatmeal
4 tbs. sugar
1 tbs. salt
4 tbs. shortening
2 pkg. dry yeast
5 1/2 cups flour
1/2 cup raisins (optional)

Add oatmeal, sugar, salt and shortening to hot water. Cool to lukewarm; add yeast and dissolve. Add one-half of the flour and beat smooth. Add raisins here and rest of flour. Beat together. Make same as white bread only let rise twice.

Bake at 375° about 50-60 min.

CORNMEAL MOLASSES BREAD

        1 1/2 cups boiling water
        1/2 cup cornmeal
        1/2 cup cold water
        1/2 cup molasses, or honey, or
                        maple syrup
        3 tbs. shortening
        2 tbs. salt
        2 pkg. dry yeast
        5-6 cups flour

Boil water, combine cold water and cornmeal and add. Cook until thick and remove from heat. Add molasses, shortening, and salt. Cool to lukewarm; add yeast and dissolve. Add flour until blended. Make same as white bread only let rise twice.

Bake at 375°. Play the piano for 55 min. and your bread will be done.

NOTE: Even non piano players can make this bread!

DARK RYE BREAD

4 cups rye flour
4 cups white flour
2 pkg. dry yeast
1/2 cup cocoa
3 tbs. sugar
5 tsp. caraway seeds
2 tsp. salt
2 1/2 cups strong black coffee OR
    water + 2 1/2 tsp. instant coffee
1/4 cup vinegar
1/4 cup dark corn syrup
1/4 cup shortening

    Place hot coffee, vinegar, corn syrup, salt, shortening, sugar, and cocoa in bowl and stir. When lukewarm add yeast and dissolve. Stir in rye flour and caraway seeds until well blended. Add white flour to make a stiff dough. (May take a little more or less than 4 cups.) Knead 5-8 min. on lightly floured board until smooth and satin finish. Place in bowl, let rise until double in bulk. Punch down and shape into loaves. Let rise until double in bulk. Bake in hot oven 400° for about 45 min. or until done.

DINNER ROLLS

2 cups hot water
1/4 cup shortening
1 tbs. salt
2 eggs beaten
2 pkg. dry yeast
1/4 cup sugar
5-6 cups flour

Place hot water in bowl. Add shortening, salt, sugar, and eggs. Cool to lukewarm. Add yeast and dissolve; add flour. Place on lightly floured surface. Knead until smooth and elastic. Let rise until double in bulk. Shape into rolls the size of golf balls. Place on buttered pan just touching each other and brush with melted butter. Let rise until double in size. Bake at 375° for 18-20 min.

This same dough may be formed into rolls the size of 2 golf balls put together for extra large rolls or dinner rolls about 4 x 4. Eat enough and you can end up the same size!

BUTTERHORN ROLLS - CLOVERLEAF ROLLS

1 1/4 cups scalded milk
5 tbs. sugar
2 tsp. salt
6 tbs. butter or margarine
2 eggs beaten
2 pkg. dry yeast
5 cups flour

Scald milk; add sugar, salt, butter, and beaten egg. Cool to lukewarm; add yeast and dissolve. Add flour and blend. Knead on a floured surface until smooth and satiny and let rise until double in bulk. Divide into two balls; roll each ball into a 10-inch circle and cut like a pie into 12 pieces and brush with melted butter. Roll from outside toward center. Place on well greased pan, butter tops, and let rise until double in size. Bake at 400° for 18 min. or until golden brown and done.

For smaller rolls, divide into 3 or 4 balls and roll into circles.

For cloverleaf rolls, make dough into balls the size of marbles. Drop 3 in each section of buttered muffin tin and let rise. Bake 15 min. at 400°.

CINNAMON ROLLS

1 1/2 cups scalded milk
1/2 cup sugar
1/2 cup shortening
2 tsp. salt
2 eggs beaten
2 pkg. dry yeast
6 cups flour

FILLING

1 cup sugar
2 tbs. cinnamon
Melted butter

Scald milk; add shortening, sugar, salt, and eggs. Cool to lukewarm; add yeast and dissolve. Add flour and blend. Knead on floured surface until smooth and satiny; let rise until double in bulk.

Place dough in long strip and flatten with hands to about 6 inches wide and 1/2 inch thick, and long. Brush with melted butter except edge nearest you so that it will stick when rolled. Spread generously with cinnamon and sugar and roll like jelly roll.

Cut in slices about 1 1/2 inches thick and place on buttered pan with slices just touching. Brush generously with butter and let rise until double in size. Bake at 375° for 20-25 min. or until done.

Left over cinnamon rolls can be frozen and will defrost sweet and moist.

Also, slice in half, butter, and slide under broiler or on a skillet until golden brown.

To reheat as rolls, just wrap in aluminum foil and set in oven for 10-15 minutes.

CHRISTMAS STOLLEN

Make Cinnamon Roll dough. Blend in 1 cup candied fruit when kneading for last time. Shape into long oval loaves and brush with butter. Let rise until almost double in bulk.

OR

Make into a braid. Bake at 375° for 30-35 minutes.

Cover with a vanilla-butter glace and decorate with candied cherries and green candied fruit.

NOTES

MAIN DISHES

" Yum Yum Yum "

MAIN MEALS

Roast Beef and Yorkshire Pudding

Roast Pork or Crown Roast

Roast Leg of Lamb

Roast Chicken or Turkey

Roast Duck

Baked Ham

Gravies

Liver and Onions

Beef Stew

Braised Short Ribs of Beef

Beef Stroganoff

Swiss Steak

Pot Roast

Pork Chops 1-2-3-4-5

Chicken and Gravy

Chicken a la King

Chicken Pot Pie

Braised Chicken Breasts

Old Fashioned Meat Loaf

Stuffed Cabbage Rolls

Swedish Meat Balls

Spaghetti and Meat Balls

American Chop Suey

Sloppy Joes

Fried Rice

Quiche Lorraine

Mushroom and Spinach Quiche

Boiled Dinner

Red Flannel Hash

ROAST BEEF AND YORKSHIRE PUDDING

Roast dry with no water. Select a roast such as rib roast, top of the round, rib eye, sometimes bottom round. Place in a pan about 2 inches deep and just enough room around the roast so that it fits into pan. Pat flour all over top of roast, fat side up. This makes a crispy, yummy crust. Add salt and pepper and place in a 400° oven for about 15 min., then reduce oven to 350° and roast about 15 min. per pound total time for rare, 18 min. per pound for medium, and 20 min. per pound for well done.

Example for a 4-pound roast:

Rare   — 1 hour
Medium   — 1 hour + 10-12 min.
Well done — 1 hour + 20 min.

If the roast is thin and not chunky, less time is required. Let roast set about 15 min. before you slice it so that the natural juices will go thru the meat. Good to have Yorkshire Pudding.

If you want oven brown vegetables such as potatoes, carrots, or onions, peel and roast and turn around meat for an hour.

YORKSHIRE PUDDING

3 eggs, 1 cup milk, 1 1/4 cup flour, 3/4 tsp. salt

Beat eggs and milk together; add flour and salt; beat until bubbles form on top. Pour into pan that the roast was cooked in with about 1/4 inch of pan drippings. Place in 425° oven for 30 min. until golden brown and set. Cut into squares and serve with roast beef.

ROAST PORK OR CROWN ROAST

Select a pork roast or fresh ham. Place in pan just a little larger than meat. Add flour, salt and pepper to the roast, also a touch of rosemary, thyme, and marjoram for a little flavor. Roast about 30 min. per pound starting in 400° oven for 15 min., then turn to 325° to finish.

For Crown Roast, have butcher prepare. Cook same as for roast only add bread stuffing or wild rice stuffing in center while roasting.

ROAST LEG OF LAMB

Place lamb in pan the same as for pork with flour, salt and pepper. Add a wedge or a few slivers of garlic in pierced sections of meat, or use a little garlic salt. Also good with slices of onion on top.

Roast in 400° oven for 15 min., then 325° oven until finished, about 20–25 min. per pound.

ROAST CHICKEN OR TURKEY

Wash and pat dry the chicken and place either on a rack or just in a roasting pan 2 in. deep and just a little larger than the bird. Pat with flour, salt and pepper, and place in a 400° oven for 15 min., then a 350° oven until done, about 20 min. per pound. Baste the bird about every 15 min.

Another method I use is to place the bird breast side down so that as it roasts the natural fats and juices go to the breast and make the white meat more moist.

If you can't baste every 15 min., just cover with foil, or cover and leave it until the last 15 min., then uncover to brown and crisp a little.

You can roast it empty or stuff it. If empty, make stuffing separately and pour a bit of the juices out of the pan near the end to give your stuffing more flavor.

ROAST DUCK

Wash and pat dry. Prick well with a fork so that the oils can come out. Pat well with flour to form a crispy crust. Salt and pepper and place on rack to keep it out of grease. Place in 400° oven for 30 min., then turn oven to 350° until done, 20 min. per lb. Prick again as duck roasts to let grease out.

ORANGE SAUCE -- Pour grease off pan. Add juice and grated coarse rind of 2 oranges. Simmer and thicken with a little cornstarch and water. Pour over duck as served.

BAKED HAM

Select a canned ham, ham slice, or whole ham. f ham is not pre-cooked, boil it for an hour starting in cold water, then drain and treat the same as for canned ham. In selecting hams, sometimes the more expensive canned ham is the best buy because there is less fat and gelatin to pay for.

Here are a few different choices for you:

1. 1/2 cup brown sugar
   1/8 tsp. ground cloves
   Enough vinegar to make it thick but not runny
   2 tsp. prepared mustard
   1 tbs. grape or currant jelly (optional)

2. 1/2 cup brown sugar
   1 small can crushed pineapple or tidbits
   1/8 tsp. ground cloves
   1/4 cup raisins (optional)

3. 1/2 cup brown sugar
   1 medium onion diced
   2 tbs. vinegar
   Dash of cloves

Score ham criss cross so that flavor bakes into ham. Place glace over ham and around it. Bake in a 350° oven for about an hour, basting every 15 min. to get a beautiful glace.

GRAVIES

For more flavor in your gravies when roasting beef, lamb, chicken, turkey, or pork, dice a few carrots, onions, and celery and roast around the meat.

Drain off fat and pour water into pan, about 1/2 to 1 cup, and bring to a boil and simmer for a few minutes. Thicken with a little flour and water and let cook for a few minutes to cook out starch flavor.

Some people use the fat from the pan with a little flour to thicken. This is all right, but very difficult to digest with the extra animal fat.

You can strain gravy or leave it with vegetables; or for poultry, dice giblets into it.

LIVER AND ONIONS

Either fry a few strips of bacon and reserve and use fat for onions, or place onions sliced into buttered pan and saute until tender. Set aside.

Dredge liver (chicken, beef, or pork) in flour, salt and pepper, and place in hot greased fry pan. Quickly brown on one side. Turn over and turn heat down and cook until juices appear at surface of liver.

Pour onions over top and serve.

BRAISED SHORT RIBS OF BEEF

8-12 short ribs of beef
3 small onions, cut in half and sliced
3 carrots, peeled and coarsely chopped
4 sticks celery, chopped
1 large can tomato puree
1 can consomme
1 tsp. sugar
Salt and pepper

Place ribs in pan which can be covered. Sprinkle with flour, salt, and pepper. Put in 425° oven until brown, about 30 min. Drain off excess fat.

Put onions, carrots, celery, puree, consomme, and sugar over top. Cover and bake for 3 hours at 350°. Uncover and bake another 30 min. until tender. Some ribs cook more quickly than others so you will have to check them after 2 hours.

Serve with vegetables over the ribs, and sauce can be poured over rice.

BEEF STEW

2 lbs. beef cut into 1-inch cubes
3 onions
6 carrots
2 pieces celery
1 cup turnip
1 cup cabbage
3-4 potatoes

Place meat in a bag or bowl with flour, salt and pepper. Coat the meat with mixture.

In the bottom of a large pot pour a little cooking oil or shortening. Heat until it just smokes. Saute beef cubes until golden brown on all sides.

Add chopped onions, celery, and just cover meat with water. Simmer for 1 hour.

Add rest of vegetables and cook for another hour until potatoes and carrots are tender but a little crisp.

Vary this according to your liking of vegetables. Salt and pepper to taste.

BEEF STROGANOFF

2 lbs. good beef, steak, top round,
      or tender cut, cut into
      1-inch cubes
4 tbs. butter
1 small onion diced
1/2 lb. sliced mushrooms
Salt and pepper
1/2 tsp. nutmeg
1/2 pt. sour cream

Brown beef quickly in a little fat in a hot skillet or pan; set aside. In another pan heat butter; add onions and mushrooms. Cook until onions are translucent and pour over beef. Add sour cream, salt, pepper, and nutmeg. Simmer for 15 min. until flavor sets through. If stroganoff thickens too much, add a little milk or water.

SWISS STEAK

Use 2 pounds of top or bottom round of beef. Cook the same as for short ribs. If you wish to shorten time, steak can be browned in fry pan and then placed in roasting pan with other ingredients and baked for only 2 hours.

POT ROAST

Use a chuck roast, shoulder, rump, or round, about 4-5 pounds. In a deep pot put a little fat and brown roast on all sides. Pour 2 cups water in with 2 carrots, 2 sticks celery, 1 onion cut in large chunks, and simmer for 3-4 hours until tender. Other vegetables--potatoes, carrots, etc.--can be added in last hour of cooking for a full meal.

PORK CHOPS

Chops cut 3/4 inch thick are better for bak-ing. Thin chops cook more quickly.

```
         6-8 pork chops
         3/4 cup chopped carrots
(1)      3/4 cup chopped onion
         3/4 cup chopped celery
         1 can condensed soup--mushroom,
              cream of celery, cream of
              chicken
      Salt and pepper
```

Brown chops on both sides in deep skillet or fry pan. Pour vegetables, salt, pepper, and soup over chops and simmer for about 45 min. until chops are tender. Add a little water if needed.

PORK CHOPS

(5) <u>Baked Stuffed Pork Chops</u>

Place 6-8 pork chops in shallow roasting pan. Place stuffing on top and bake at 350° for 1 1/2 hours, or until tender depending on thickness of chops--1 hour for thin chops.

<u>Stuffing</u> - Mix 2 cups bread crumbs
Salt and pepper
2 eggs
1/2 cup water
1 small onion
2 tsp. poultry seasoning
1 diced apple (optional)

CHICKEN AND GRAVY

One 4-5 pound roasting chicker
or fowl
2 carrots, chopped
2 sticks celery, chopped
2 medium onions, chopped

Almost cover bird with water and add vegetables in a large pot. Boil for 2 1/2-3 hours or until bird almost falls off bones. Remove chicken and continue to boil liquid and vegetables until stock is reduced by half.

Pick meat off bones and set aside. Strain stock and save vegetables.

CHICKEN AND GRAVY (Continued)

Put 6 tbs. butter in pan and simmer. Add 7 tbs. flour and stir until blended with a whisk or beater. Add this mixture to 6 cups of boiling stock and simmer on low heat until thick and starch taste has cooked out. Add salt, pepper, cut up chicken meat, and vegetables if you want. Add to sauce and serve on rice, mashed potatoes, or hot fluffy tender biscuits.

CHICKEN a la KING

To chicken and gravy mixture, add 1 small can diced pimento, 1/4 pound sliced and fried mushrooms, 1 small green pepper, sliced and tossed with mushrooms, and 2 tbs. sherry (opt.)

CHICKEN POT PIE

Add any left over vegetables, or cook some potatoes and carrots, drain, add to chicken and gravy. Cover with flaky tender crust in a casserole and bake at 375° for 30-45 min. until crust is done.

6 chicken breasts
1/2 cup chopped celery
1/2 cup chopped carrots
1/2 cup chopped onions
Salt and pepper
1 can cream of chicken soup

Chop celery, carrots, and onions. Place in bottom of a baking dish that will hold the chicken. Place chicken on vegetables, skin side up. Spread soup over chicken and on vegetables. Bake uncovered for 1 hour. Add a little water if chicken seems to be getting dry. Turn chicken and baste to keep golden brown and moist. Bake about 1 1/2 hours total at 350° or until tender. Serve with vegetables and sauce spooned over chicken.

OLD FASHIONED MEAT LOAF

1 1/2 lb. ground beef
4 slices dry bread soaked in 1/2 c. milk
2 eggs
1 small onion diced and sauted in butter
Salt and pepper
1 can tomato soup

Place dry bread in bowl, add eggs, milk, soup, salt, pepper, and cooked onions. Blend until moist and mixed. Blend in ground beef and shape into loaf. Bake at 350° for 45 min. to 1 hr.

Can be varied by using mushroom soup or cream of celery soup.

Use this same mixture for meat balls.

STUFFED CABBAGE ROLLS

8 large cabbage leaves
2 cups ground beef
1 small onion diced
1 small green pepper
1 tsp. salt
1/2 tsp. pepper
1/2 cup cooked rice
1 large can tomatoes
Shake of Worcestershire sauce

Place cabbage leaves in boiling water for 2 min.; drain and set aside. Blend beef, onions, pepper, salt and pepper, and cooked rice and place large spoonfuls on each leaf and fold in. Place stuffed rolls in a baking dish and pour tomatoes over them. Bake at 375° for 50 min.

SWEDISH MEAT BALLS

1 lb. ground beef
1/2 lb. ground pork
1 small onion diced
1 cup bread crumbs
1 tbs. parsley
Salt and pepper
1/2 tsp. nutmeg
2 eggs
1/2 cup milk or light cream

Mix together and shape into balls. Cook in hot oil; transfer to serving dish. Use pan drippings with a little milk, bring to boil, thicken with a little flour and water. Pour over meat balls. Garnish with chopped parsley.

SPAGHETTI AND MEAT BALLS

    1 small onion
    1 large can tomato puree
    1 small can tomato paste
    2 cloves garlic minced
    1 tsp. salt
    1/2 tsp. pepper
    1 tsp. sugar
    1/4 tsp. oregano
    1 bay leaf

Saute onion, garlic, and rest of ingredients and simmer for 3 hours. Add meat balls from meat ball recipe. Simmer for awhile so that the sauce taste will go through the meat balls.

Cook spaghetti; rinse in cold water to prevent sticking; pour hot water over it to keep hot.

If you add a little oil to your water while cooking spaghetti, it will not stick together as quickly, if at all.

AMERICAN CHOP SUEY

    1 lb. hamburg
    1 medium onion
    1 large can tomatoes
    Salt and pepper
    1 cup raw macaroni cooked

Saute onion; add hamburg and brown; add tomatoes and cook for few minutes just on simmer. Add cooked macaroni, salt and pepper. Serve then or place in casserole dish, sprinkle with cheese, crumbs, butter, and heat in 350° oven for 15-20 min.

SLOPPY JOES

1 lb. hamburg
1 small onion
1 can tomato soup
1 cup beef bouillon
Salt and pepper
1 tsp. Worcestershire sauce

Saute onion; add hamburg and brown. Add all other ingredients and simmer 10-15 min. Thicken with a little flour and water to thickness desired. Serve on a bun.

FRIED RICE

1 tbs. shortening
1 large onion
1 large pepper
Few mushrooms (optional)
1 cup diced left over meat
2 eggs
3 tbs. soy sauce
3 cups cooked rice--firm but don't
over cook

In large skillet or wok, stir in hot fat onions, pepper, mushrooms. Add raw egg and stir thru to make streaks. Add meat, rice, and Soy sauce. Keep turning until blended and hot.

QUICHE

Line pie plate with flaky tender crust. Add, beaten together,

> 1 1/2 cups milk (some cream
>   for richer flavor)
> 4 eggs
> Salt and pepper

and pour into shell. Add 3/4 cup grated cheese, Swiss or Parmesan or a mixture of cheeses.

Sprinkle cooked crisp bacon on top OR chopped spinach and sliced raw mushrooms.

Bake at 375° for 45 min. or until knife comes out clean.

BOILED DINNER

4 - 5 pounds corned beef or a smoked shoulder
6 carrots, cut in lengths
6 onions, peeled
1 turnip, peeled and sliced
6 potatoes, peeled
1 head cabbage, wedged
6 beets, washed and whole or
   1 can small whole beets

Place meat in a large pot and cover with cold water. Bring to a boil and then simmer for 3 to 4 hours, or until tender. Add all the vegetables and simmer for one more hour.

Serve on a large platter as a one-dish meal.

Cook enough extra vegetables and make Red Flannel Hash the next day.

RED FLANNEL HASH

Take all the vegetables left over from your boiled dinner and chop them together, the beets giving you the red color. If you like, you may grind the meat and add in also.

Pan fry in a little butter and, for extra flavor, brown up a diced onion before adding hash.

May be served with a poached egg if desired.

Vegetables

VEGETABLES

Asparagus

Baked Vegetables

Baked Beans

Green Bean Casserole

Harvard Beets

Cauliflower

Fried Cabbage

Egg Plant

Egg Plant Parmesan

Sauted Mushrooms

Stuffed Mushrooms

Baked Potatoes

Baked Stuffed Potatoes

Mashed Potatoes

Scalloped Potatoes

Lyonnaise Potatoes

Parsley Boiled Potatoes

Candied Sweet Potatoes

Creamed Onions (New England)

Dry Squash

Hubbard Squash

Turnip

Fried Tomatoes - Red or Green

Scalloped Tomatoes

Broiled Tomatoes

Zucchini Squash

Stuffed Zucchini

Corn on the Cob

Corn Pudding

Carrots and Turnip

Cold Pickled Beets

Dandelion Greens

Fiddleheads

ASPARAGUS

Trim lower part of stalks and keep bright green end. Wash well. Place in boiling water with a little salt and cook until tender. Drain; serve with butter, salt and pepper, or Hollandaise sauce.

BAKED VEGETABLES

If you want a treat, bake your vegetables. You not only retain all the flavor, but you save room on top of your stove if you have other things going. I bake the following:

Asparagus   Carrots
Broccoli   Onions
Brussels Sprouts   Summer Squash
Cabbage

Wash vegetables; peel if necessary; place in a covered casserole dish. Dot with butter, salt, pepper, and 2 tbs. water. Cover tight and bake at 375° for about 30 min. or until tender. The smaller the vegetables are cut or sliced, the more quickly they will cook.

BAKED BEANS

1 lb. dry beans
1 tsp. dry mustard
1/2 tsp. salt
1/4 lb. salt pork
1/2 cup molasses
1 tbs. brown sugar
2 tbs. catsup
2 small onions, sliced

Wash beans several times. Soak over night in fresh clear water. Place in bean pot or covered dish or pot. Add all the ingredients and just barely cover with water. Stir together. Cover; bake for about 8 hours at 350°. Leave uncovered the last hour. Add water as the beans cook if necessary.

GREEN BEAN CASSEROLE

Place frozen green beans, cooked fresh beans, or canned beans in a buttered casserole. Mix in 1 can mushroom soup. Dice onions and place a layer 1/4 - 1/2 inch thick over top. Cover with bread crumbs and melted butter. Bake in a 375° oven for 30-45 min. or until golden brown.

HARVARD BEETS

1/3 cup beet juice, or water if
        using fresh beets
1/3 cup vinegar
1/2 cup sugar
1 tbs. cornstarch
1 tbs. butter
1/8 tsp. cloves
Salt and pepper

Bring liquids and sugar to a boil; thicken with a little water and cornstarch. Add salt, pepper, cloves, and butter. Add beets. Keep warm until ready to serve.

CAULIFLOWER

Cut head into separate pieces. Place in boiling salted water and cook until tender. Add milk to water to keep cauliflower whiter.

Excellent with a mild cheese sauce or creamed sauce.

FRIED CABBAGE

Dice salt pork and fry until brown and crispy. Remove from fat. Add chopped cabbage and fry until tender but crisp. Add pork scraps, salt and pepper.

EGG PLANT

Cut in 1/2 inch thick slices. Peel skin. Dip in flour, egg, and crumbs. Fry on both sides in butter until tender. Add salt for seasoning.

EGG PLANT PARMESAN

Placed peeled egg plant, sliced 1/2 inch thick, in buttered casserole. Cover with Spaghetti sauce and top with Parmesan cheese. Bake in 350° oven 30-40 min.

SAUTED MUSHROOMS

Wash mushrooms well. Slice and place in hot butter. Turn until golden brown.

STUFFED MUSHROOMS

Select large mushrooms. Cut stems out and chop fine. Add 1 egg, 1 small diced onion, 2 tbs. flour, 1 tbs. cream, salt and pepper. Blend and stuff back into caps. Brush with butter and place in 425° oven for 10-12 min. If mixture seems thin, add some Ritz cracker crumbs.

BAKED POTATOES

Set oven to 450°. Select large potatoes, wash, prick with fork to let out steam. Place on rack in oven and bake for 45 min. or until tender. If you are baking other things in oven at 350°, allow almost 2 hours for potatoes.

BAKED STUFFED POTATOES

Follow above instructions. When done, cut in half lengthwise and scoop potato into bowl. Add butter, salt and pepper, a little milk, and either chopped chive or bacon. Whip together. Spoon back into skin, brush with butter, and top with grated cheese. Use now or heat when ready in hot oven for a few minutes. Can be done ahead for a party and refrigerated.

MASHED POTATOES

Peel potatoes and just cover with water. Boil until tender. Drain well; add salt, pepper, and butter. Mash, add milk, and beat until light and fluffy. Too little milk will make potato dry and stiff.

SCALLOPED POTATOES

Alternate several layers thin sliced raw peeled potatoes with thin sliced onion in buttered casserole. Sprinkle with flour, salt, and pepper on each potato layer. Dot with butter and pour milk over to almost cover layers. Bake at 400° for about 45 min. or until tender.

LYONNAISE POTATOES

Slice one medium onion and saute in butter until slightly transparent. Add cooked sliced potatoes and cook with salt, pepper, and onion until heated and golden brown.

PARSLEY BOILED POTATOES

Boil peeled potatoes until tender. Chop parsley; add to melted butter. Pour over drained potatoes.

CANDIED SWEET POTATOES

Boil sweet potatoes in skins until tender. Do not overcook because sweet potatoes may get mushy. Peel skins off. Set in buttered casserole. Sprinkle brown sugar and melted butter over them. Brown in hot oven for 15 min.

CREAMED ONIONS (New England)

Boil sliced onions until tender. Drain well. Add cream, butter, salt and pepper.

DRY SQUASH
Butternut, Buttercup, and Dry Squash

Peel skin and remove seeds. Barely cover with water. Boil until tender. Drain well. Add lots of butter, salt, pepper, and milk enough to make it smooth and creamy. One squash may take 1/2 – 1 cup of milk.

HUBBARD SQUASH

Cook the same as for Dry squash. Drain well and add salt, pepper, and butter. Also, if squash seems watery, add 1 tbs. cornstarch dissolved in a little milk. This will just take up the slack in a moist squash.

TURNIP

Peel, cut into small pieces, and barely cover with water. Boil until tender. Drain well. Add 1 tbs. brown sugar to each small turnip, plus butter, salt and pepper.

FRIED TOMATOES - RED OR GREEN

Slice 1/2 inch thick. Coat with flour. Dip in a little beaten egg and coat with fine bread or cracker crumbs. Pan fry until golden brown in a little shortening.

SCALLOPED TOMATOES

1 can tomatoes
2 slices dry bread
1 small onion diced
Pinch of allspice
2 shakes of Worcestershire sauce
1 tsp. sugar

Mix all together. Add some crumbs on top Dot with butter. Bake at 350° for 35-40 min. or until golden brown.

BROILED TOMATOES

Cut ripe tomatoes in half. Add salt, pepper, Parmesan cheese, and dot with butter. Broil for a few minutes until golden brown.

ZUCCHINI SQUASH

In a heavy sauce pan, cut Zucchini into small slices. Add fresh tomatoes, onion, and green pepper. Simmer for 1 to 1 1/2 hours. Add Parmesan cheese, salt, pepper, and butter.

STUFFED ZUCCHINI

Slice 6 small squash lengthwise. Scoop out most of the center and dice. Dice one medium onion and one small clove of garlic. Add 1 pound ground lamb or beef, salt and pepper. Spoon the whole mixture, including squash, back into the scooped out squash. Place in buttered casserole and bake 35-45 min. at 375°.

Anyone could add rice to mixture and cover with tomato sauce for a change.

CORN ON THE COB

Start with the freshest corn possible. The best way would be to pick it and boil it over an open fire right in the corn field. Next would be to boil it in the house for 4 to 5 min. Do not salt water because it could make corn shrivel. Some people add a little milk to the water.

If you have a Microwave oven, place husked corn in plastic wrap or bag and cook for 2 min. per ear. You will have to decide how crisp or well done you like your corn.

Use left over corn for corn chowder, corn pudding, or add to basic muffin. Remember to remove it from cob.

CORN PUDDING

2 cups left over corn off the cob or
   1 can kernel corn
1 1/4 cups of milk
2 eggs
2 tbs. flour
1/2 tsp. salt
Dash of pepper
3 tbs. melted butter

Butter a casserole dish. Beat eggs, add milk, salt, pepper, and flour and beat until smooth. Add corn and melted butter and stir together.

Pour into casserole and bake at 350° for about 1 hour, or until knife will come out clean.

Set casserole dish in pan of hot water when baking for a less crispy bottom layer.

CARROTS AND TURNIP

Slice or cut vegetables into bite size pieces. Just cover with water and cook until just tender.

Drain any water off and sprinkle with brown sugar. Add butter and a dash of lemon juice and serve, salt and pepper to taste.

A favorite vegetable served at Uncle Don Drew's Westcustogo Inn.

COLD PICKLED BEETS

1 cup vinegar
1/3 cup sugar
Dash of ground cloves
Salt and pepper
Sliced raw onion (optional)
1 can drained beets or
   1 1/2 - 2 cups sliced cooked beets

Mix together and set overnight—better after 1 - 2 days.

DANDELION GREENS

Clean fresh, small greens several times in water. The best greens are picked where there are no cats or dogs.

Cook in boiling water with a small piece of salt pork, or butter. Lower heat and simmer for about 45 min. Drain and add salt, pepper, butter, and lemon juice or vinegar.

FIDDLEHEADS

Wash fiddleheads well, rinsing several times. Place in a covered pan with 1 tbs. water, just enough to steam and cook on low heat 10 to 15 min. Do not over cook.

Add salt, pepper, and butter. Some like lemon juice or vinegar also.

"Oh Yaaa"

VEGETABLE AND MEAT SAUCES

Basic White or Cream Sauce

Cheese Sauce

Hollandaise Sauce

Bearnaise Sauce

Egg Sauce

Tartar Sauce

Sweet Salad Mustard

Cocktail Sauce

BASIC WHITE SAUCE OR CREAM SAUCE

2 tbs. butter
2 tbs. flour
1 cup scalded milk
Salt and pepper

Heat milk in double boiler. Add cooked butter and flour using a whisk or beater to keep it smooth. Add salt and pepper. Cook about 10-12 min. until raw flour taste is gone.

CHEESE SAUCE

Add 1/2 cup shredded Cheddar cheese and melt in basic white sauce.

HOLLANDAISE SAUCE

4 egg yolks
1 tbs. lemon juice
1/2 cup water
1/2 cup melted butter
1/4 tsp. salt
Dash of pepper

Beat with whisk egg yolks, lemon juice, and water. Place in a pan over boiling water and beat until thick. Add melted butter in stream, beating constantly. Add salt and pepper.

Do not overheat or it will separate. If too thick, a little cream may be added. Keep warm, but not hot, until ready to serve.

BEARNAISE SAUCE

Add to Hollandaise Sauce 1 1/2 tsp. chopped parsley, 1 tsp. chopped tarragon (or a little tarragon vinegar,) and a dash of onion salt.

EGG SAUCE

Make Cream Sauce and add chopped hard boiled eggs. A little chopped parsley adds a pretty touch.

TARTAR SAUCE

1 cup mayonnaise
4 olives, stuffed and diced fine
4 tbs. chopped dill pickle
2 tsp. chopped parsley
1 tbs. sweet relish

Blend together and serve.

SWEET SALAD MUSTARD

2 eggs beaten
1/2 cup sugar
4 tbs. dry mustard
1/2 cup cream
1/2 cup vinegar
2 tbs. butter

In a double boiler, mix eggs, sugar, mustard, and cream until smooth. Add vinegar and butter and cook for 15 min., stirring until thick.

Store in a jar in the refrigerator.

COCKTAIL SAUCE

1/2 cup catsup
1 tsp. Worcestershire Sauce
1 tsp. horseradish (more if desired)
1 tsp. lemon juice
1/4 tsp. black pepper
3 drops Tabasco Sauce

Mix together and serve with Seafoods.

NOTES

PASTRIES

FLAKY TENDER CRUST

PASTRIES AND PIES

Flaky Tender Pie Crust
Apple Pie
Apple Crunch Pie
Blueberry Pie
Raspberry Pie
Peach Pie
Rhubarb Pie
Strawberry Pie
Pineapple Meringue Pie
Vanilla Cream Filling
Graham Cracker Pie
Banana Cream Pie
Coconut Cream Pie
Cream Pies—Fresh Strawberry, Blueberry,
              Raspberry, Peach
Chocolate Cream Pie
Butterscotch Cream Pie
Lemon Meringue Pie
Meringue
Two-Crust Lemon Pie
Lemon Sponge Pie
Chocolate Nut Delight
Pecan Pie
Angel Pie—Lemon or Chocolate
Eggnog Chiffon Pie
Strawberry or Raspberry Chiffon Pie
Custard Pie
Pumpkin or Squash Pie
Glaced Fruit Pies—Strawberry, Raspberry,
                    Peach
Strawberry Glace Cheesecake
Apple Pan Dowdy
Cobblers
Baked Maine or (Alaska)
Butter Almond Raspberry Pie
Mocha Cheese Cake
Cranberry Pie

FLAKY TENDER PIE CRUST

1 Crust Pie	2 Crust Pie
1/4 tsp. salt	1/2 tsp. salt
2 tbs. + 2 tsp. water	5 tbs. + 1 tsp. water
1/3 cup lard or white shortening	2/3 cup lard or white shortening
1 cup flour	2 cups flour

Place flour and salt in bowl. Work lard in with fork, knives, or fingers, leaving the lard in pieces the size of peas. Add water and stir with fork until all flour is taken in and one lump of crust is formed.

Roll on well floured surface so that the shortening that breaks through will not stick to counter or rolling pin. If done by this method your crust will always be flaky and tender. Any white firm shortening can be used but I like lard for a real flaky crust. When rolling pie crust, roll as thin as possible for bottom crusts to prevent them from being too soggy. This crust can be used on all recipes calling for pie crust.

For added color always brush tops of pies with a little egg and milk, like 1 egg and 4 tbs. milk.

When making two-crust pies, always keep lip of pie from any sugar or filling because this prevents a good seal and your pie will leak and run over.

PIE CRUST (Continued)

After your filling is in, wet with water the complete rim. Set top crust on and firm with palms of hands, then if you want to crimp the edge with a fork, go ahead. Vent the pie with a slash in the middle.

For one-crust pies, always prick the crust well on bottom and sides to prevent it from rising in humps.

I bake all my pies at 375° until golden brown and crust separates slightly from pan in a sealed pie.

APPLE PIE

	8 apples
Blend	(3/4 cup sugar
	(3/4 tsp. cinnamon
	(1 tbs. flour
	(1/8 tsp. salt

Slice peeled apples into bottom shell; sprinkle sugar, cinnamon, salt, and flour over apples. Wet edge of pie. Top with crust. Bake at 375° for 45 min. to 55 min., or till golden brown and apples are tender.

APPLE CRUNCH PIE

8 apples

Blend
(3/4 cup brown sugar
(1/4 cup butter
(1/4 cup flour
(1/8 tsp. salt
(1/8 tsp. cinnamon

Slice apples into one shell. Top with crunch mixture and bake open in 375° for 45 min.

BLUEBERRY PIE

2 1/2 - 3 cups blueberries, fresh
or frozen

Blend
(1/2 cup sugar
(1 tbs. flour
(1/4 tsp. cinnamon
(1/8 tsp. salt

Place blueberries in shell. Cover with mixture. Wet edges and top with crust. **Bake at** 375° for 45-55 min.

RASPBERRY PIE

3 cups fresh raspberries

Blend
(3/4 cup sugar
(2 tbs. flour
(1/8 tsp. salt

Place berries in shell. Cover with mixture. Wet edges. Place top crust on and bake at 375° for 50-55 min.

PEACH PIE

8 peaches, more if small, OR 2 cups
          drained cling peaches
1/4 cup brown sugar
1 tbs. flour
2 tbs. butter
Dash of nutmeg adds a little touch

Place peaches in shell; cover with sugar and flour. Dot with butter. Wet edges and cover with top crust. Bake at 375° for 45-55 min.

RHUBARB PIE

2 1/2 - 3 cups cut rhubarb
(1 cup sugar
Blend (1/8 tsp. salt
(2 tbs. flour

Pour boiling water over rhubarb and drain. Mix with BLEND and place in pie shell. Wet edges. Place top crust on and bake at 375° for 50-55 min. (Boiling water takes out any bitterness in rhubarb.)

STRAWBERRY PIE

2 1/2 cups sliced strawberries
(1/2 cup sugar
Blend (2 tbs. flour
(1/8 tsp. salt

Make same as for Raspberry Pie.

PINEAPPLE MERINGUE PIE

1 1/2 cups milk
1/2 cup sugar
1/8 tsp. salt
2 tbs. cornstarch
3 egg yolks
1 cup well drained pineapple
1/2 tsp. vanilla

Meringue

3 egg whites
3 tbs. sugar
1 tbs. water
Pinch of cream of tartar
Pinch of salt

Place milk in double boiler and heat until it begins to skim on top. Mix sugar, salt, cornstarch, and egg yolks together and stir into hot milk. Cook until thick. Cool a little. Add pineapple and vanilla. Pour into baked pie shell and cover with meringue.

MERINGUE: Beat egg whites and water until stiff. Add cream of tartar, salt, and sugar, 1 tbs. at a time, and beat well. Cover pie with meringue and sprinkle 1 level tbs. sugar over top of pie. This will give a beautiful golden brown pie and make it cut more easily.

Bake in a 375° oven for 3-5 min. Watch carefully because it will brown quickly.

(A copper mixing bowl will increase the volume of meringue. Always use clean utensils)

VANILLA CREAM FILLING

2 cups milk
2 eggs
1/2 cup sugar
3 tbs. cornstarch
1/8 tsp. salt
1 tbs. butter
1 tsp. vanilla

Place milk in double boiler and heat until it skims on top. Beat eggs, sugar, cornstarch, and salt. Add to hot milk and stir until thick and it coats spoon. Add vanilla and butter. Cool for a while; pour into pie shell and chill. Sugar may be reduced to 1/4 cup if you prefer a pie less sweet. This is the base pudding for the following pies.

GRAHAM CRACKER PIE

Make a graham cracker crust and fill with Vanilla Cream Pudding. Top with meringue or whipped cream.

BANANA CREAM PIE

Slice bananas into a baked flaky tender pie shell. Cover with Vanilla Cream Pudding and top with whipped cream. Trim with sliced bananas when ready to serve.

COCONUT CREAM PIE

Add 1/2 cup shredded cocoanut to Vanilla Cream Pudding. Pour into baked flaky tender pie shell. Top with whipped cream and dust with toasted cocoanut.

CREAM PIES - Fresh Strawberry, Blueberry,
Raspberry, Peach

Slice 1 cup strawberries, peaches, or berries
into the bottom of a baked tender flaky pie shell.
Pour Vanilla Cream Pudding over. Top with cream
whipped and decorate with fruit on top.

CHOCOLATE CREAM PIE

Melt 2 squares of chocolate in double boiler.
Add to Vanilla Cream Pudding. Pour into baked
tender flaky pie shell. Top with whipped cream.

BUTTERSCOTCH CREAM PIE

1 cup brown sugar
1/4 cup cornstarch
1/2 tsp. salt
2 1/2 cups milk
3 egg yolks
1/3 cup butter
1 1/2 tsp. vanilla

Heat 2 cups milk in double boiler until it skims
on top. Add butter and melt. Mix brown sugar,
cornstarch, salt, egg yolks, and 1/2 cup milk.
Add to hot milk and cook until thick. Add vanilla.
Cool slightly. Pour into baked flaky tender crust
and top with meringue.

LEMON MERINGUE PIE

Juice and rind of 2 lemons
2 tbs. butter
1 1/2 cups hot water
1 1/2 cups sugar
4 egg yolks
3 tbs. flour

Heat water and butter in double boiler. Mix sugar, juice and rind of lemons, egg yolks, and flour. Add to hot water. Cook until thick and raw taste is gone from flour. Cool slightly. Spoon into baked flaky tender pie shell. Top with meringue from 4 egg whites, 4 tbs. sugar, and 1 tbs. plus 1 tsp. water, and 1/8 tsp. cream of tartar. Follow directions for Meringue.

MERINGUE

For a perfect meringue, start with a clean, grease-free bowl. A copper bowl (if you have one) will increase the volume due to the reaction of the egg whites and the copper.

4 egg whites
4 tsp. water
1/8 tsp. cream of tartar
4 tbs. sugar
Dash of salt

Beat whites and water until stiff, but not dry. Add cream of tartar and salt, and sugar 1 tbs. at a time. Beat in. When finished the meringue should have a satin luster. Top pie with the me-ringue, bringing it out to meet the crusts. This prevents shrinking from edges. Bake in a 325° oven until golden brown, about 12 min. or so.

TWO-CRUST LEMON PIE
(Extra special rich)

2 cups sugar
2 lemons, juice and rind
3 beaten eggs
2 tbs. water
1/3 cup melted butter

Place all ingredients except butter in bowl and beat smooth. Add melted butter and beat again. Pour into pie shell, wet edges well, cover gently with top crust. Press edges firm, brush with egg wash. Bake at 375° for 50-60 min.

LEMON SPONGE PIE

1 cup sugar
2 tbs. butter
2 eggs separated
2 tbs. flour
1 lemon, juice and rind
1 cup milk

Mix sugar, butter, flour, egg yolks, lemon juice and rind. Add milk and mix. Fold in stiff egg whites and pour into unbaked flaky tender pie shell. Bake at 350° for 30-40 min. until golden brown and cake springs back to touch.

CHOCOLATE NUT DELIGHT

1 cup flour
3/4 cup sugar
1 tsp. baking powder
1/2 tsp. salt
1/4 cup butter
1/2 cup milk
2 eggs
1 tsp. vanilla

SAUCE

Bring to
boil

(1 square chocolate
(1/2 cup water
(2/3 cup sugar

Add

(1/4 cup butter
(1 tsp. vanilla

1/4 cup chopped nuts

Place all ingredients in bowl and beat until smooth and blended. Pour into unbaked flaky tender pie shell and pour Sauce over top. Top with nuts and bake at 350° for 30-40 min. until cake springs back. Top with whipped cream or ice cream.

PECAN PIE

4 eggs
3/4 cup brown sugar
1 cup dark Karo syrup
4 tbs. melted butter
1 tbs. flour
1/4 tsp. salt
2 tsp. vanilla
1 cup pecans

Beat eggs, sugar, Karo, butter, flour, salt and vanilla. Pour into unbaked pastry shell. Sprinkle nuts over top. Bake at 375° for 40-45 min. until it puffs, is golden brown, and knife cuts clean. Serve with whipped cream or ice cream.

ANGEL PIE - Lemon or Chocolate

5 egg whites
1 cup sugar
1/4 tsp. cream of tartar

2 tbs. water
5 egg yolks
1/2 cup sugar
1 lemon, juice and rind
1 cup whipped cream

Beat egg whites and cream of tartar until stiff. Beat in 1 cup sugar gradually. Spread in well-greased pie pan. Bake at 275° for 1 hour until light brown but dry. If not dry, turn oven off and leave pie in until dry.

ANGEL PIE (Continued)

Beat egg yolks until thick and lemon co
Beat in sugar, juice and lemon rind, and w
Cook in double boiler until thick. Cool and
filling over angel crust. Top with whipped

For a change, add chopped nut meats t
ringue when baking. Make one-half recipe
Chocolate Pie Filling for center and top wi
whipped cream.

EGGNOG CHIFFON PIE

2 tsp. gelatin
1/4 cup cold water
4 egg yolks
1 cup milk
1/2 cup sugar
1/8 tsp. salt
1 1/2 tsp. vanilla
4 egg whites
1/2 cup whipped cream
1 tsp. nutmeg
2 tbs. rum (optional)

Dissolve gelatin in cold water. Heat
double boiler. Add beaten egg yolks, gel
ture, sugar and salt. Stir until thick. C
add vanilla. When cool enough and starts
fold in beaten egg whites, cream, nutmeg
rum. Pile into baked flaky tender pie sh
and serve with whipped cream or plain c
You may dust top with a little extra nutm

STRAWBERRY OR RASPBERRY CHIFFON PIE

2 cups berries (slice strawberries)
3/4 cup sugar
4 tsp. gelatin
1/4 cup cold water
1/2 cup boiling water
3 egg whites
1/8 tsp. salt

Place 1 cup berries on bottom of baked flaky tender pie shell. Dissolve gelatin in cold water. Add boiling water, sugar, salt, and dissolve. Place rest of berries in mixture and chill until it begins to thicken. Beat egg whites until stiff. Fold into mixture and pour over berries in shell. Chill until set. Serve with whipped cream and a few berries on top for decoration.

CUSTARD PIE

3 cups milk
5 eggs
1/2 cup sugar
1/4 tsp. salt
1 tsp. nutmeg
1 tsp. vanilla

Place everything in a bowl and beat until well blended. Pour into unbaked flaky tender pie shell and bake at 400° for 10 min. Reduce heat to 350° until custard sets and knife comes out clean, for 30-40 min. more.

PUMPKIN OR SQUASH PIE

1 cup cooked squash or pumpkin
2 cups milk (part cream or evapo-
        rated milk for a rich pie)
1 cup brown sugar
4 eggs (beaten)
1 tsp. cinnamon
1 tsp. nutmeg
1/2 tsp. ginger
1/2 tsp. salt

Mix all ingredients together. Pour into pie
shell and bake as for Custard Pie.

GLACED FRUIT PIES
Strawberry, Raspberry, Peach

3 cups fruit for large pie
3/4 cup sugar
1/2 cup water
2 tbs. cornstarch
1/4 cup water
Dash of salt

Bring sugar, salt, water, and 1/2 cup sliced
fruit to a boil. Cook until fruit is cooked, about
10 min. Pour mixture through strainer, crush-
ing fruit through. Return mixture to stove and
thicken with cornstarch and water. Place rest
of fruit in baked flaky tender shell. Pour hot
mixture over fruit. Chill and serve with small
splashes of whipped cream.

STRAWBERRY GLACE CHEESECAKE

1 graham cracker crust

4 eggs
1 lb. cream cheese
2/3 cup sugar
1 tsp. vanilla
2 tbs. lemon juice

Blend
(2 cups sour cream
(1/2 cup sugar
(1 tsp. vanilla

GLACE

1 pkg. frozen berries
2 tbs. cornstarch
1/4 cup water
1 tsp. lemon juice

Soften cream cheese; add sugar, vanilla, lemon juice. Beat until smooth. Add eggs and beat until blended. Pour into graham shell and bake at 375° about 20 min. until it puffs, cracks, and is just starting to brown.

Have sour cream, sugar, vanilla blended and ready. Remove cheese cake from oven. Pour mixture gently over it. Return to oven for 10 more minutes. Cool until set.

GLACE: Drain berries. Bring juice to a boil. Thicken with cornstarch and water. Cook until clear. Add berries and pour over cold cheese cake. This makes a large pie or something like a 9 x 12 or similar size.

APPLE PAN DOWDY

8 apples peeled, cored, and sliced
1 cup brown sugar
1/4 cup melted butter
1 tsp. lemon juice
1 tbs. flour
1 recipe for flaky tender crust

Place sliced apples in square tin. Cover with sugar and flour, mixed. Dribble melted butter and lemon juice over apples. Cover with top crust. Bake at 375° for about 45 min., or until crust is golden brown and apples are bubbling at edges. Serve warm with a big scoop of vanilla ice cream.

COBBLERS

4 tsp. sugar
1 3/4 cups flour
2 1/2 tsp. baking powder
1/2 tsp. salt
5 tbs. shortening
1/2 cup + 1 tbs. milk

Mix flour, baking powder, sugar, and salt. Blend in shortening until the size of peas. Add milk and mix until all ingredients are together. Roll on floured board about 1/4 inch thick. Place over any fruit mixture. Sprinkle top with a bit of sugar. Bake at 375° about 45–50 min.

Fruit Mixture
Place fruit in pan. Sprinkle with sugar and a little flour. Cover with cobbler crust and bake until light, fluffy, and golden brown.

BAKED MAINE OR (ALASKA)

Use Flaky Tender Crust, cooked, or Angel Cake, Pound Cake, or Sponge Cake.

Use an oven-proof platter or pie plate that you will serve on.

Place Crust, or Cake, on bottom of platter. Cover with layers of your favorite Ice Creams or all the same flavor. Leave 1/2 inch space around the edges.

Cover all the Ice Cream with Meringue, probably a double recipe, down to the Crust, or Cake, so that no Ice Cream is exposed.

Swirls and designs with pastry bags may be made, but remember that tall peaks may burn before the rest browns over.

Place in 450° oven for 2 to 3 min. until golden brown. Serve immediately or return to freezer.

You may prepare everything and place in freezer until ready to bake in oven.

Serve with chocolate sauce, strawberries, or your favorite sauce or fruit.

Also, you may slice fresh fruit over Ice Cream before you cover with Meringue.

BUTTER ALMOND RASPBERRY PIE
(Was a Favorite at
Uncle Don Drew's Westcustogo Inn)

1 cup flour
3/4 cup sugar
1 tsp. baking powder
1/2 tsp. salt
1/4 cup butter
1/2 cup milk
2 eggs
1 tsp. Almond extract
1 cup Raspberry filling or heavy jam

Cream butter, sugar, and Almond extract. Add eggs and beat. Add dry ingredients and milk and blend.

Make one unbaked Flaky Tender Pie Crust shell. Spread filling over bottom and pour batter on top.

Bake 375° for 30-40 min. until cake part springs back.

Serve with whipped cream or ice cream.

MOCHA CHEESE CAKE

4 eggs
1 lb. cream cheese
2/3 cup sugar
1 tsp. vanilla
2 tbs. lemon juice
2 squares melted chocolate

Blend (2 cups sour cream
      (1/2 cup sugar
      (1 tsp. vanilla

Dissolve and (1 tbs. Instant coffee
  add   (1 tbs. Hot water

Soften cream cheese; add sugar, vanilla, and lemon juice. Beat until smooth. Add eggs and beat until blended. Pour into Graham Cracker shell and bake at 375° about 20 min. until (it puffs, cracks, and is starting to brown on edges.)

Have sour cream mixture blended and ready. Remove cheese cake from oven and pour mixture gently over it. Return to oven for 10 more min. Remove and cool.

CRANBERRY PIE

2 cups cranberries
1 cup raisins
1 1/2 cups sugar
2 tbs. flour
1 orange, juice and grated rind
3/4 cup boiling water
1/4 tsp. salt

Mix flour, sugar, orange rind, and salt. Add boiling water, orange juice, and blend. Add cranberries and raisins and stir together.

Bake in 2 Flaky Tender Crusts at 375° for 45-55 min., or until golden brown and berries are tender.

Desserts and Puddings

Hm m m m m!

PUDDINGS AND DESSERTS

Apple Crisp

Apple Brown Betty

Rhubarb Crisp

Vanilla Custard Bread Pudding

Chocolate Custard Bread Pudding

Coffee Tapioca Supreme

Grapenut Custard

Plain Custard

Indian Pudding

Mocha Nut Chip Mousse

Mocha Pudding Cake

Snow Pudding

Custard Sauce

Cream Puffs and Filling

Jelly Roll or Ice Cream Roll

Chocolate Roll

Baked Apples

Old-Fashioned Rice Custard

APPLE CRISP

8 apples peeled, cored, and sliced
1/2 cup sugar
1/2 tsp. cinnamon

Topping (1/2 cup brown sugar
(1/2 cup flour
(1/4 cup butter

Place sliced apples in buttered baking dish. Sprinkle sugar and cinnamon over them. Blend topping ingredients together and spread over top of apples. Bake at 350° for 45 min. or golden brown.

APPLE BROWN BETTY

8 apples peeled, cored,
and sliced
1 cup bread crumbs
4 tbs. melted butter
1/2 cup brown sugar
1 tsp. cinnamon
1/4 tsp. salt
1/2 cup hot water

Mix crumbs and butter together. Place a few in bottom of baking dish; add layer of apples. Sprinkle with sugar and cinnamon. Repeat, ending with a few crumbs on top lightly dusted with sugar. Pour water and salt over top. Bake at 350° 40 min.

RHUBARB CRISP

3 cups rhubarb
1 1/2 cups sugar
1 tbs. flour
1/2 cup brown sugar
1/2 cup flour
1/4 cup butter

Cut rhubarb. Pour boiling water over it and drain. Place in buttered baking dish and mix in sugar and 1 tbs. flour. Mix flour, sugar, and butter. Spread evenly over top. Press in several places to firm. Bake in 350° oven for 45 min. or golden brown and bubbly.

VANILLA CUSTARD BREAD PUDDING

3 cups milk
3 eggs
1 1/2 cups dry bread crumbs
1 tsp. vanilla
1/2 tsp. nutmeg
1/2 tsp. salt
3/4 cup sugar

Beat eggs; add milk, sugar, salt, vanilla and nutmeg. Beat until blended. Place crumbs in buttered baking dish. Pour mixture over them. Poke bread down to completely moisten. Bake with pan set in water, if possible, for 1 hour at 350°. Serve with Hard Sauce or Nutmeg Sauce.

CHOCOLATE CUSTARD BREAD PUDDING

Follow directions for Vanilla Pudding. Add 2 squares melted chocolate or use 2 1/2 cups milk and 1/2 cup hot water with 6 tbs. cocoa mixed in. Serve with Hard Sauce or Whipped Cream.

COFFEE TAPIOCA SUPREME

4 cups hot black coffee
1/2 scant cup quick cooking tapioca
1/2 tsp. salt
1 cup sugar
1/4 cup slivered almonds, toasted (optional)
2 cups whipped cream or Cool Whip
2 tsp. vanilla

Pour the coffee into a double boiler. Add sugar, salt, and tapioca. Cook until tapioca is clear. Chill. Fold in whipped cream, vanilla, and slivered almonds.

GRAPENUT CUSTARD

3 cups milk
5 eggs
3/4 cup sugar
1/2 tsp. salt
1 tsp. vanilla
1 cup grapenuts

Beat eggs; add milk, sugar, salt, and vanilla. Beat until blended. Pour into buttered baking dish sprinkle grapenuts over top. Bake at 350° for about 1 hour until knife comes out clean. Bake in a pan of water as an underliner for best results.

PLAIN CUSTARD

Same as for Grapenut Custard except omit grapenuts.

INDIAN PUDDING

3 cups scalded milk
1 cup cold milk
1/3 cup dark molasses
1/3 cup sugar
1/3 cup cornmeal
1/2 tsp. cinnamon
1/4 tsp. salt
1/2 tsp. nutmeg
3 tbs. butter

Scald milk in double boiler. Add molasses. Mix sugar, cornmeal, cinnamon, nutmeg, and salt. Add to scalded milk and cook until thickened. Add butter. Pour into buttered baking dish. Add cold milk--just pour over it. Bake in a slow oven 300° for 2 hours or until a knife comes out clean. This is the old fashioned way. You can't rush good Indian Pudding. Serve with vanilla ice cream or whipped cream.

A yummy treat. I describe the taste as a cross between a pumpkin pie and a molasses cookie.

PLAIN CUSTARD

Same as for Grapenut Custard except omit grapenuts.

INDIAN PUDDING

3 cups scalded milk
1 cup cold milk
1/3 cup dark molasses
1/3 cup sugar
1/3 cup cornmeal
1/2 tsp. cinnamon
1/4 tsp. salt
1/2 tsp. nutmeg
3 tbs. butter

Scald milk in double boiler. Add molasses. Mix sugar, cornmeal, cinnamon, nutmeg, and salt. Add to scalded milk and cook until thickened. Add butter. Pour into buttered baking dish. Add cold milk--just pour over it. Bake in a slow oven 300° for 2 hours or until a knife comes out clean. This is the old fashioned way. You can't rush good Indian Pudding. Serve with vanilla ice cream or whipped cream.

A yummy treat. I describe the taste as a cross between a pumpkin pie and a molasses cookie.

MOCHA NUT CHIP MOUSSE

1 pkg. plain gelatin
3/4 cup hot coffee
2 cups chocolate pudding
1 cup whipped cream
1/2 cup chopped nuts
1/2 cup chocolate chips
1 tsp. vanilla

Dissolve gelatin in coffee. Chill until thick but not firm. Place in bowl. Add pudding and whipped cream and beat until smooth. Fold in chips, nuts, and vanilla. Chill until firm. Makes a good filling for a pie if you add an extra package of plain gelatin to coffee.

MOCHA PUDDING CAKE

3/4 cup sugar
1 cup flour
2 tsp. baking powder
1/8 tsp. salt
1 square chocolate
3 tbs. butter
1/2 cup milk
1 tsp. vanilla

Topping
(1/2 cup brown sugar
(1/2 cup white sugar
(4 tbs. cocoa
(1 cup cold black coffee

Mix dry ingredients together. Add milk and vanilla. Melt chocolate and butter together. Add and beat. Pour into greased baking pan. Add blended sugars and cocoa on top. Pour coffee over top. Do not stir mixtures together in baking dish. Bake at 350° for 40 min. Great with vanilla ice cream.

SNOW PUDDING

1/4 cup cold water
1 pkg. plain gelatin
1 cup boiling water
3/4 cup sugar
Juice and rind of 1 lemon
2 egg whites beaten stiff

Dissolve gelatin in a little cold water. Add boiling water and dissolve. Add sugar, juice and rind. Chill until it starts to set. Beat in egg whites until whole mixture is frothy and light. Chill until firm. Serve with Custard Sauce.

CUSTARD SAUCE

1 cup scalded milk
2 egg yolks
1/4 cup sugar
1/2 tsp. cornstarch
1/2 tsp. vanilla

Cook until it coats spoon. Add vanilla. Serve warm.

CREAM PUFFS

1 cup water
1/2 cup shortening (butter for a
                              richer puff)
Dash salt
1 cup flour
3 eggs

Boil water, shortening, and salt together. Add flour and stir until mixture cooks and leaves side of pan. Beat in eggs, one at a time. Drop on baking sheet and bake at 450° for 15 min. Reduce heat to 350° for 15-20 min. Makes 12.

CREAM PUFF FILLING

2 cups scalded milk
2 eggs
1/2 cup sugar
2 tbs. cornstarch
1 tbs. butter
1 tsp. vanilla

Scald milk in double boiler. Add beaten eggs, sugar, and cornstarch. Cook until thick. Remove from heat. Add vanilla and butter.

For eclairs, place batter in long 1/2" round lengths. To fill, split with knife and spoon in filling.

JELLY ROLL or ICE CREAM ROLL

5 egg whites
1 cup sugar
5 egg yolks
1 1/2 tsp. vanilla
1 1/2 tbs. real lemon juice
1 1/2 tbs. water
1 cup sifted flour
1 1/4 tsp. baking powder
1/4 tsp. salt

Beat egg whites until stiff. Beat in 1/4 cup sugar and set aside. Beat egg yolks until thick. Add rest of sugar, vanilla, water, and lemon juice. Pour this mixture over the whites. Fold in until blended. Sift flour, baking powder, and salt. Fold gently into egg mixture. Do not beat.

JELLY ROLL - (Continued)

Grease shallow pan 12 x 20. Line with waxed paper. Grease again. Spread mixture evenly and bake in a 375° oven until light golden and tests done to touch (springs back.)

Turn on to a towel sprinkled with confectioner's sugar. Pull off paper and cut thin strips from edges to make it roll without breaking. Roll the cake in the towel and let set for 5 min. or so. Un-roll, spread with filling or ice cream. Roll up again and set aside. If using ice cream, put in freezer.

CHOCOLATE ROLL

Substitute 1/4 cup cocoa for 1/4 cup flour. Use 3 tbs. water and no lemon juice.

BAKED APPLES

Wash and core number of apples to use. Place in a baking dish and add a mixture of 1/2 cup sugar and 2 tsp. cinnamon to the center of apple. Place 1/2 cup water in pan and cook in 400° oven 20 to 30 min. until tender. Baste 2 or 3 times.

Serve with cream.

OLD-FASHIONED RICE CUSTARD

3 cups milk
4 eggs
1 cup sugar
1/2 tsp. salt
1 1/2 tsp. vanilla
1 1/2 cups cooked Rice
1 cup raisins

Beat eggs, milk, sugar, salt and vanilla until blended. Pour into buttered casserole dish. Add rice and raisins and stir. Set dish in a pan of hot water as an underliner, and bake at 350° for 1 hour to 1 1/4 hours until knife comes out clean.

WHAT DID YOU EXPECT?

CAKES

Angel Cake

Chocolate Angel Cake

Apple Upside Down Cake

Banana Cup Cakes

Butter Sponge Cake

Blueberry Cake

Cherry Nut Cake

Chocolate Chip Layer Cake

Chocolate Custard Layer Cake

Devil's Food Cake

Harlequin Birthday Cake

Hot Milk Cake

Maple Nut Cake

Marble Cake

Spice Cake

Velvet Luncheon Cake

Hot Chocolate Cake

Gingerbread

Tomato Soup Cake

Carrot Cake

Red Velvet Cake

Ice Cream Cake

ANGEL CAKE

12 egg whites
1 1/2 tsp. cream of tartar
3/4 tsp. salt
1 1/2 cups sifted sugar
1 tsp. vanilla extract
1 tsp. almond extract
1 cup sifted flour

Beat egg whites until frothy. Add salt and cream of tartar. Beat stiff. Beat in 1 cup sugar and flavoring. Fold in flour sifted three times with 1/2 cup sugar. Bake in Angel Cake ring, ungreased, for 50 min. at 325°, and 10 min. more at 300°. Invert pan on rack and leave for about an hour.

CHOCOLATE ANGEL CAKE

Substitute 1/4 cup cocoa for 1/4 cup flour and leave out almond. Save yolks for a Butter Sponge Cake, custard, or Hollandaise Sauce.

APPLE UPSIDE DOWN CAKE

1/4 cup butter
3/4 cup brown sugar
1 3/4 cup tart sliced apples

Melt butter in bottom of 8 x 8 pan. Mix in brown sugar and cover with sliced apples.

(Continued)

154

APPLE UPSIDE DOWN CAKE - (Continued)

Batter

1 1/4 cups flour
1 1/4 tsp. baking powder
1/4 tsp. salt
2 eggs
1 cup sugar
1 tsp. vanilla
5 tbs. boiling water

Beat eggs until thick and light colored. Add sugar and beat well. Add vanilla. Sift all dry ingredients together and add alternately with boiling water by folding in lightly. Pour over apples. Bake at 350° for 50 min. Turn out onto platter. Garnish with vanilla ice cream or whipped cream.

BANANA CUP CAKES

1/2 cup shortening
1 1/2 cups sugar
2 beaten eggs
2 cups flour
1/2 tsp. salt
1 tsp. baking powder
3/4 tsp. baking soda
1/4 cup sour milk
1 cup mashed bananas
1 tsp. vanilla

Cream shortening and sugar; add eggs. Mix dry ingredients and add alternately with sour milk. Add mashed bananas and vanilla. Drop into cupcake pans and bake at 375° about 20 min. Makes 2 1/2 doz. Also makes a good layer cake. Tastes mighty good with coffee icing.

BUTTER SPONGE CAKE

12 egg yolks
2 cups sifted sugar
1 cup scalded milk
1 tsp. lemon extract
1/2 tsp. orange extract
2 1/4 cups sifted flour
2 tsp. baking powder
1/2 tsp. salt
1/2 cup melted butter

Beat yolks with sugar until light and fluffy. Add milk and extracts, then flour sifted with baking powder and salt. Fold in melted butter. Bake in two greased 8 x 8 pans at 350° for 30–40 min., or in angel ring for about 1 hour at 350°. Use egg whites for Angel Cake, French Bread, or Meringue for a pie.

BLUEBERRY CAKE

3/4 cup sugar
1/4 cup shortening
1 tsp. vanilla
2 eggs
1 1/3 cups flour
2 tsp. baking powder
1/4 tsp. salt
1/2 cup milk
1 cup blueberries

TOPPING   (1/4 cup sugar
(1/2 tsp. cinnamon

(Continued)

BLUEBERRY CAKE - (Continued)

Cream sugar and shortening until light and fluffy. Add eggs and beat. Add extract. Add sifted dry ingredients alternately with milk. Fold in 1 cup blueberries. Sprinkle top with Topping. Bake in 9 x 9 pan at 350° for 25-30 min.

CHERRY NUT CAKE

1/2 cup shortening
1 1/4 cups sugar
2 eggs
3/4 tsp. almond extract
2 1/2 cups flour
3 1/2 tsp. baking powder
1/2 tsp. salt
1 cup milk
1/2 cup chopped cherries
1/2 cup nuts

Cream shortening and sugar. Add eggs and extract. Sift dry ingredients and add alternately with milk. Fold in nuts and cherries. Bake at 350° for 45 min. in 12 x 8 x 2 pan or layer cake pan. A thin glace complements this cake.

CHOCOLATE CHIP LAYER CAKE

1 1/4 cups brown sugar
1/4 cup white sugar
1/2 cup shortening
3 eggs
2 cups flour
3 tsp. baking powder
1 tsp. salt
1/2 tsp. soda
1 1/4 cups milk
2 tsp. vanilla
1/2 cup chocolate chips

Cream shortening and sugar. Add eggs and vanilla. Sift dry ingredients and add alternately with milk. Fold in chocolate chips and bake in layer cake pans for 20-25 min. at 350°.

FILLING: Scald 1/2 cup milk. Add 2 tbs. flour, 1/4 cup brown sugar. Cook until thick. Add 2 tbs. butter, 1/4 cup nuts, and 1 tsp. vanilla. Cool and spread between layers. Frost with butter cream or chocolate icing.

CHOCOLATE CUSTARD LAYER CAKE

1/2 cup shortening
1 cup sugar
1/2 cup cocoa
1 egg
1/2 cup sour milk
1 1/2 cups flour
1 tsp. baking soda
1/4 tsp. salt
1/2 cup hot water
1 tsp. vanilla

Cream shortening and sugar. Add cocoa and egg and beat. Add vanilla. Add baking soda dissolved in sour milk and some dry ingredients. Sift remaining dry ingredients and add alternately with hot water. Bake at 350° for 20-25 min.

FILLING

1 cup scalded milk
1/2 cup sugar
1 egg
1/2 tbs. cornstarch
1 tbs. butter
1 tsp. vanilla

In double boiler add sugar, egg, and cornstarch to scalded milk and cook until thick. Cool, add butter and vanilla. Spread between layers and frost with butter glace.

DEVIL'S FOOD CAKE

1 3/4 cups flour
1 1/4 tsp. baking powder
1/2 tsp. baking soda
1 tsp. salt
2 squares melted chocolate
1 1/2 cups sugar
1/2 cup shortening
1 cup milk
2 eggs.

Mix dry ingredients together. Add shortening and milk. Beat for 2 min. Add eggs and chocolate and beat for 2 more min. Bake at 350° 45-50 min.

The true Devil's food color came from adding red food coloring in the old days. If a harmless red coloring is manufactured, use it.

HARLEQUIN BIRTHDAY CAKE

3/4 cup shortening
2 cups sugar
1 tsp. salt
3 cups flour
4 tsp. baking powder
1 1/4 cups water
5 egg whites beaten stiff
1 tsp. vanilla

Cream shortening and sugar. Add extract. Sift dry ingredients and add alternately with water. Fold in beaten egg whites. Divide into 3 parts. Leave one white. Add 2 tbs. cocoa to one and a little pink coloring to the other. Bake in 3 layers at 375° for 20 min. or until done. Frost with butter cream or chocolate icing.

HOT MILK CAKE

2 eggs separated
1 cup sugar
1 cup flour
2 tsp. baking powder
1/2 tsp. salt
1 tsp. vanilla
1/2 cup hot milk

Beat egg whites until stiff. Add yolks, beat. Add sugar and extract and beat. Mix dry ingredients and add. Last add hot milk. Bake at 350° for 35-40 min.

MAPLE NUT CAKE

1/2 cup shortening
1 cup brown sugar
2 eggs separated
1 tsp. maple flavor or vanilla
extract
1/2 cup milk
1 1/2 cups flour
1/4 tsp. salt
2 tsp. baking powder
1/2 cup nuts

Cream shortening and sugar. Add egg yolks and extract. Add milk and dry ingredients. Fold in beaten stiff egg whites and 1/2 cup nuts. Bake at 375° for 35-40 min.

MARBLE CAKE

2 cups flour
3 tsp. baking powder
1 tsp. salt
1 1/2 cups sugar
1/2 cup shortening
1 cup milk
2 eggs
1 tsp. vanilla

Place all dry ingredients in bowl. Add shortening and milk and beat for 2 min. Add eggs and
vanilla and beat for 2 min. more. Divide batter
in half. Add 3 tbs. cocoa to one-half. Place
white and chocolate batter alternately in pan and
swirl with knife. Bake at 375° for 30-35 min.

SPICE CAKE

1/2 cup shortening
1 cup brown sugar
2 eggs
1/2 cup sour milk
1/2 tsp. baking soda
1/2 tsp. baking powder
1 1/3 cups flour
1/2 tsp. nutmeg
1/2 tsp. cloves
1/2 tsp. cinnamon
1/4 tsp. salt

Cream shortening and sugar. Add eggs. Sift
dry ingredients and add alternately with sour milk
and soda blended. Bake at 350° for 30-40 min.

VELVET LUNCHEON CAKE

        1 cup sugar
        1/2 cup butter
        1 egg separated
        1 cup sour milk with 1 tsp. baking
            soda dissolved in it
        1/2 tsp. salt
        3/4 tsp. nutmeg
        1/2 tsp. cinnamon
        1 tsp. lemon extract
        1 3/4 cups flour
        1 cup chopped raisins
        3/4 cup nuts

Cream shortening and sugar. Add egg yolk and lemon extract. Add all dry ingredients alternately with milk. Add nuts and raisins. Fold in stiffly beaten egg white. Bake at 350° for 40-50 min. or until it tests done.

HOT CHOCOLATE CAKE

        2 cups flour
        2 cups sugar
        6 tbs. cocoa
        1 tsp. salt
        1/2 cup liquid shortening
        2 eggs
        1 cup sour milk
        2 tsp. baking soda
        1/2 cup hot water
        1 1/2 tsp. vanilla

(Continued)

Mix together flour, sugar, cocoa, and salt. Add liquid shortening, beaten egg, sour milk in which soda has been added. Mix well. Add hot water and vanilla. Blend until smooth. Pour into two layer pans or one 8 x 14 pan.

This is a very thin cake batter so don't be surprised. You will look a long way to find such a dark, moist cake. Great with a vanilla or coffee butter glace. Serve warm with whipped cream.

In olden days this was called a Husband Catcher Cake because it was so good that any girl a-courtin could win her bo!

GINGERBREAD

1/2 cup shortening
1/2 cup sugar
1 cup molasses
2 3/4 cups flour
1 1/2 tsp. cinnamon
1 tsp. nutmeg
3/4 tsp. cloves
1 tsp. ginger
1 tsp. salt
2/3 cup hot water
2 1/2 tsp. baking soda
3 eggs

Cream shortening and sugar. Add molasses and beat. Add all dry ingredients alternately with hot water and baking soda blend. Add beaten eggs. Bake at 350° for 30 min. or until it tests done. Serve with whipped cream or lemon sauce.

TOMATO SOUP CAKE

2 cups flour
1 tsp. baking powder
3/4 cup raisins
1/4 cup melted shortening
1 can condensed tomato soup
1 cup sugar
1 tsp. baking soda
1 tsp. cinnamon
1/2 tsp. nutmeg
1/4 tsp. cloves
1/4 tsp. salt
1 egg beaten

Mix flour, baking powder, soda, salt, and spices. Stir raisins into flour to coat them. Mix melted shortening, egg, sugar, and soup. Add this to dry ingredients and mix well.

Bake in 8 x 4'' loaf pan, or 8 x 8'' pan at 350° for around an hour.

CARROT CAKE

2 cups sugar
3 cups flour
2 tsp. baking soda
2 tsp. baking powder
2 tsp. cinnamon
1/2 tsp. salt
1 1/2 cups oil
4 eggs
2 1/2 cups grated carrots
1 cup walnuts
1/2 cup raisins (optional)

Mix all dry ingredients in bowl. Beat eggs and oil together and mix into dry ingredients and blend well. Add carrots, nuts, and raisins.

Bake in buttered tube pan for 1 hour, or in a 9 x 13" pan for about the same time.

This is a very moist cake and may need a little more time in oven. Test—Frost with Cream Cheese Icing.

RED VELVET CAKE

1/2 cup butter
1 1/2 cups sugar
2 eggs
2 oz. red food coloring
1 tbs. cocoa
1 tsp. salt
1 cup sour milk or buttermilk
2 1/4 cups flour
1 tsp. baking soda
1 tsp. vinegar
1 tsp. vanilla

Cream shortening, sugar, and cocoa. Add eggs, vanilla, and salt and beat. Add food coloring. Add one half the flour, one half the milk, then repeat. Mix vinegar and baking soda and mix in last.

Bake in two 9-inch pans for 30 min. at 350°.

Frost with butter cream or cream cheese frosting.

ICE CREAM CAKE

1/2 cup butter
2 cups Ice Cream (any flavor)
2 eggs
2 cups flour
1 cup sugar
1 tbs. baking powder
1/2 tsp. salt
1/2 cup milk
1 tsp. vanilla

Stir butter and ice cream until soft and blended. Add all ingredients and mix together.

Bake at 350° for 35 min. Frost with your favorite frosting.

This is a moist cake with a solid texture.

NOTES

COOKIES

Banana Oatmeal Chip Nuggets

Brown Sugar Crisps

Brown Sugar Brownies

Brownies

Butter Balls

Chocolate Chip Cookies

Ice Box Cookies

Peanut Butter Cookies

Carrot Cookies

Oatmeal Cookies

Old-Fashioned Soft Molasses Cookies

Drop Sugar Cookies

Squash Cookies

Whoppie Pies

Filled Cookies

Gingerbread Kids

Thin Butter Cookies

Lemon Squares

BANANA OATMEAL CHIP NUGGETS

1 1/2 cups flour
1 cup sugar
1 tsp. baking soda
1 tsp. salt
1 tsp. nutmeg
3/4 tsp. cinnamon
3/4 cup shortening
1 egg
1 cup mashed bananas
1 3/4 cups oatmeal
1 cup chocolate chips
1/2 cup nuts (optional)

Mix dry ingredients. Cut in shortening. Add beaten egg and mashed bananas. Blend. Add oatmeal, chips, and nuts. Drop by spoonful on a greased cookie sheet. Bake at 350° for 12-15 min., or until they test done to touch and are golden in color. A real healthful cookie!

BROWN SUGAR CRISPS

1 cup brown sugar
1 cup shortening
1 egg
1 tsp. vanilla
2 cups flour
1/2 tsp. salt
1 tsp. baking soda
1 tsp. cream of tartar

Cream shortening and sugar. Add egg and vanilla. Add flour, salt, baking soda, and cream of tartar. Drop by spoonful on greased cookie sheet. Bake at 375° for 10-12 min., or until golden brown

COOKIES

Cookies are fun to make. For a cookie that is rich, tasty, and spreads to a thin crisp cookie, butter or margarine should be used. Any white shortening is good, but you will see the difference.

The larger the cookie dropped, the larger the finished cookie. I drop batter the size of a golf ball and get a large cookie. If you bake a lot of cookies, get a number 40 ice cream scoop to scoop them out from batter or dough.

BROWN SUGAR BROWNIES

1 1/3 cups brown sugar
1/3 cup shortening
2 eggs
1 2/3 cups flour
1/2 tsp. baking powder
1/2 tsp. salt
2 tsp. vanilla
1/2 - 1 cup chocolate chips
1/2 cup chopped nuts

Cream shortening and sugar. Add eggs, then flour, baking powder, salt, and vanilla. Blend. Add chips and nuts. Spread 3/4 inch thick in a good size tin. Bake at 350° until it puffs up and then drops down, about 25-30 min.

Butter or margarine makes a nicer or richer square than a regular shortening.

BROWNIES

1 cup sugar
2 eggs
1/3 cup butter or margarine
2 squares melted chocolate
1/2 cup flour
1/8 tsp. salt
1 1/2 tsp. vanilla
3/4 cup chopped nuts

Beat eggs and sugar. Add melted butter and chocolate. Add vanilla, flour, salt, and nuts. Spread 3/4 inch thick in baking tin. Bake at 350° 25-30 min.

BUTTER BALLS

1/2 lb. butter
1/2 cup confectioner's sugar
2 1/4 cups flour
1 1/2 tsp. vanilla
1 cup nuts

Blend ingredients together. Shape into balls the size of a nickel. Bake at 250° for 45 min. Roll in confectioner's sugar while warm, and again when ready to serve.

CHOCOLATE CHIP COOKIES

1 cup butter
1 cup brown sugar
1/2 cup white sugar
2 eggs
1 tsp. baking soda
2 tsp. water
1 tsp. vanilla
2 1/4 cups flour
1 pkg. chocolate chips
1/2 cup chopped nuts

Blend butter and sugar. Add eggs and rest of ingredients except nuts and chips. Stir until well blended. Add nuts and chips. Drop by spoonful on greased tin. Bake at 375° for 10-12 min., or until golden brown.

ICE BOX COOKIES

1/2 cup shortening
1/2 cup brown sugar
1/2 cup white sugar
1 egg
2 cups flour
1/2 tsp. soda
1/4 tsp. salt
1 tsp. vanilla
1/2 cup chopped nuts

Cream shortening and sugar. Add eggs and rest of ingredients. Make into a roll and wrap in waxed paper. Chill 3 to 4 hours. Slice thin and bake at 400° for a few minutes.

PEANUT BUTTER COOKIES

1/2 cup butter
1/2 cup peanut butter
1/2 cup brown sugar
1/2 cup white sugar
1 egg
1/2 tsp. soda
1 cup flour
1 tsp. vanilla

Blend sugars, butter and peanut butter. Add egg and rest of ingredients. Drop by spoonful on greased cookie sheet. Press flat with fork. Bake at 375° for 8-10 min. or until golden brown. Remove from pan and cool. Cookies get crispy as they cool.

CARROT COOKIES

1 cup shortening
3/4 cup brown sugar
1 cup mashed cooked carrots
2 eggs
2 cups flour
2 tsp. baking powder
1/2 tsp. salt
3/4 cup shredded coconut or chopped
nuts or mixture of two

Blend shortening and sugar. Add carrots, eggs, and rest of ingredients. Drop on greased baking sheet. Bake at 375° for 10-12 min. or until done to touch. Frost with Orange Butter Glace. Makes 4 dozen 2-inch cookies.

OATMEAL COOKIES

1/2 cup brown sugar
1/2 cup white sugar
1/4 lb. butter or margarine
1 egg
1/2 tsp. salt
1 cup flour
1/2 tsp. soda
1 cup dry oatmeal
1/2 cup raisins (optional)
1/2 cup nuts (optional)

Cream shortening and sugars. Add egg and rest of ingredients and blend. Drop by spoonful on greased cookie sheet. Bake at 375° for 10-12 min. or until golden brown. Undercook for chewy cookies--Longer for crispy cookies.

OLD-FASHIONED SOFT MOLASSES COOKIES

2 eggs
1/2 cup sugar
1/2 tsp. salt
1/2 tsp. ginger
1/4 tsp. cinnamon
1/4 tsp. cloves
1/2 cup lard or white shortening
1/2 cup molasses
2 tsp. baking soda
1/2 cup sour milk
3 1/2 to 4 cups flour to make stiff
  dough but able to drop from spoon

Mix eggs, sugar, salt, spices, lard, and molasses. Add flour, milk, and baking soda. Mix until smooth. Drop by spoonful on greased cookie sheet. Bake at 375° for 10-12 min., or until puffed, cracked, and spring back to touch like a cake would.

DROP SUGAR COOKIES

1 cup shortening
1 cup sugar
2 eggs
2 tsp. vanilla
2 1/4 cups flour
1/2 tsp. baking soda
1/2 tsp. salt

Cream shortening and sugar. Add egg and rest of ingredients. Drop by spoonful on greased cookie sheet. Bake at 375° for 10-12 min., or until a bit golden in color, not too brown.

SQUASH COOKIES

1 1/4 cups brown sugar
1/2 cup shortening
2 eggs
1 1/2 tsp. vanilla
1 1/2 cups cooked squash
2 1/2 cups flour
4 tsp. baking powder
1/2 tsp. salt
3/4 tsp. nutmeg
3/4 tsp. cinnamon
1/4 tsp. cloves
1/4 tsp. ginger
1 cup raisins
1/2 cup nuts

Cream shortening and sugar. Add eggs, vanilla, and squash. Add rest of ingredients except raisins and nuts and blend. Add raisins and nuts. Drop by spoonful on greased cookie sheet. Bake at 375° for 12–15 min. or until they spring back and are golden brown.

WHOOPIE PIES

4 cups flour
3 tsp. baking soda
1/2 tsp. salt
8 tbs. cocoa
2/3 cup shortening
2 cups sugar
2 eggs
2 cups milk
2 tsp. vanilla

Combine all ingredients and mix well. Drop by rounded dessert spoon (larger if you wish) on to ungreased cookie sheet. Bake 375° for 8 - 10 min. until they spring back to touch, or toothpick comes out clean. Cool and fill between two cakes.

FILLING

1 cup shortening
2 cups powdered sugar
1 cup marshmallow fluff

Place all ingredients together and beat at high speed until very fluffy. If too stiff, a little water may be added.

(Use homemade marshmallow from Frostings and Sauces)

FILLED COOKIES

1 cup sugar
1/2 cup shortening
1 egg
1/2 cup milk
2 1/2 cups flour
1 tsp. baking soda
2 tsp. cream of tartar
1 tsp. vanilla or lemon extract

Cream shortening and sugar, add egg and mix. Add rest of ingredients. Roll out thin (1/8'') on floured surface.

Cut one Large cookie, put a teaspoon of your favorite jam or filling on and place another cookie on top; press edges together.

Bake 375° from 10 to 12 min., or golden brown.

GINGERBREAD KIDS

1 cup shortening
1 cup sugar
1/2 tsp. salt
1 egg
1 cup molasses
2 tbs. vinegar
5 cups flour
1 1/2 tsp. baking soda
1 tbs. ginger
1 tsp. nutmeg
1 tsp. cloves
1 tsp. cinnamon

Cream shortening and sugar; add salt, eggs, molasses, and vinegar and beat until smooth. Add all dry ingredients and mix well.

Chill about 2 hours and roll out 1/8'' thick. Cut with cookie cutters. Bake at 375° about 6-8 min.

THIN BUTTER COOKIES

1 cup butter
3/4 cup sugar
1 egg yolk
1 tbs. cream
1/2 tsp. almond extract
2 cups flour

Cream butter and sugar. Add egg yolk, cream, and almond and beat together. Add flour.

Roll thin (1/8'') on floured surface, keeping dough just stiff enough to handle. Cut with favorite cutters and bake 6-10 min. at 400° until edges just start to get golden brown.

This works well with a Cookie Press also.

LEMON SQUARES

CRUST — 1 cup flour
1/2 cup butter, soft
1/4 cup confectioner's sugar
FILLING — 1 cup granulated sugar
2 eggs
Juice and rind of 1 lemon
1/2 tsp. baking powder
1/4 tsp. salt

Mix ingredients for crust and press into 8 inch square pan. Bake for 20 min. at 350°.

Beat all ingredients for filling until light and fluffy and pour over crust. Return to oven and bake for 25 min. or until set firm. Cook, sprinkle with confectioner's sugar, and serve.

Frostings and Dessert Sauces

" ONE STREAM OF VANILLA "

FROSTINGS AND DESSERT SAUCES

Everyday Cream Icing

Chocolate Icing

Mocha Icing

Peanut Butter Icing

Vanilla Butter Glace

Coffee Glace

Orange Glace

Cream Cheese Icing

Nutmeg Sauce

Lemon Sauce

Orange Sauce

Hard Sauce

Hot Fudge Sauce

Hot Butterscotch Sauce

Quick Butterscotch Sauce

Custard Sauce

Blueberry or Fruit Sauce

Marshmallow

Rich Chocolate Frosting

EVERYDAY CREAM ICING

2 cups confectioner's sugar
1 egg white
2 tbs. water
1 tsp. extract (vanilla, lemon, orange, etc.)
1/3 cup white shortening or butter

Stir by hand confectioner's sugar, egg white, extract, and water until stiff but still able to stir. Add either a little more water or sugar if not just right. Add shortening and beat until light and fluffy. This could be a little heavy for a small hand mixer but a table model should do all right.

This should spread smoothly, hold its shape, and taste yummy.

For decorating icing, just add a little more sugar for stiffness.

CHOCOLATE ICING

Use Everyday Icing but add 3 tbs. cocoa when adding sugar.

MOCHA ICING

Follow Chocolate recipe and use black coffee in place of water or 1 tsp. instant coffee.

PEANUT BUTTER ICING

Follow recipe for Everyday Icing only substitute 3 tbs. peanut butter and 2 tbs. shortening in place of 1/3 cup shortening.

VANILLA BUTTER GLACE

A thin rich icing for tasty cakes that shouldn't be hidden with thick frostings.

> 1 cup confectioner's sugar
> 1 tbs. melted butter
> 2 tbs. water
> 1/2 tsp. vanilla

Mix together over a touch of heat until lukewarm to the touch—should just run enough to spread over cake evenly. Overheating will make it dull and cracky. Should be smooth and have a satiny finish.

COFFEE GLACE

Same as above only add 1 tsp. instant coffee, or substitute strong black coffee for water.

ORANGE GLACE

> 1 cup confectioner's sugar
> Juice and rind of 1 orange
> 1 tbs. melted butter

Follow directions for Vanilla Butter Glace.

CREAM CHEESE ICING

2 cups confectioner's sugar
1 egg white
5 tbs. cream cheese
1 tsp. vanilla

Beat all ingredients together until smooth and fluffy.

NUTMEG SAUCE

1 cup boiling water
1/2 cup sugar
1 tbs. cornstarch
3 tbs. butter
1 tsp. vanilla
1 tsp. nutmeg
Dash of salt

Boil water. Add sugar and cornstarch combined. Stir for 4-5 min. on low boil until thick and clear. Remove from heat. Add vanilla, nutmeg, salt, and butter. Try it on blueberry cake or bread custard pudding.

LEMON SAUCE

1 cup boiling water
1/2 cup sugar
1 tbs. cornstarch
3 tbs. butter
Juice and rind of 1 lemon
Dash of salt

Bring water, juice, and rind to a boil. Add sugar and cornstarch combined. Boil 4-5 min. until thick and clear. Remove from heat. Add butter and salt.

ORANGE SAUCE

Same as for Lemon Sauce except use only all orange juice for liquid, and rind of orange instead of lemon. Tasty on Peach Pancakes.

HARD SAUCE

1 cup confectioner's sugar
1/3 cup butter
1 tsp. vanilla OR 2 tsp. brandy

Work together until well blended. Chill. Serve on Custard Bread Puddings.

HOT FUDGE SAUCE

1 cup sugar
1/3 cup cocoa
2 tbs. flour
1 tsp. salt
1 cup boiling water
1 tbs. butter
1 tsp. vanilla

Cook all ingredients except butter and vanilla on low heat until thick, stirring constantly, or in a double boiler. Add butter and vanilla.

HOT BUTTERSCOTCH SAUCE

1 lb. brown sugar
1/3 cup butter
3 tsp. lemon juice
1/2 cup cream or milk

Cook in double boiler for 45-50 min. until thick. Add 1 tsp. vanilla.

QUICK BUTTERSCOTCH SAUCE

3/4 cup brown sugar
3/4 cup Karo syrup
3 tbs. butter
1 cup milk or cream
1 tsp. vanilla

Combine sugar, syrup, and butter. Cook for 5 min. Add milk or cream. Bring to boil. Remove from heat. Add vanilla.

CUSTARD SAUCE

1 cup scalded milk
2 egg yolks
1/4 cup sugar
1/2 tsp. cornstarch
1/2 tsp. vanilla

Combine sugar, cornstarch, and egg yolk. Add to scalded milk and cook until it coats spoon. Add vanilla.

BLUEBERRY OR FRUIT SAUCE

    1 cup fruit
    1/4 cup sugar
    1/2 cup water
    1 tbs. cornstarch in a little
                   water
    1/2 tsp. cinnamon (for blue-
               berries)

Combine fruit, sugar, and water. Bring to boil and simmer for 1 min. Add cornstarch and water. Cook until clear and slightly thickened. Add cinnamon (for blueberries.) Thickness regulated by more or less cornstarch. May use other fruits such as raspberries, strawberries, and peaches.

MARSHMALLOW

    3 tsp. plain gelatin
    1/3 cup water
    2 1/2 cups confectioner's sugar
    4 egg whites
    1 cup light Karo syrup

Soak gelatin in cold water for 5 min. Heat until dissolved. In mixing bowl place confectioner's sugar, egg whites, Karo, and gelatin-water mixture. Beat with electric mixer for 10 min. until light, fluffy, and firm.

Keep in refrigerator and beat again if separation occurs.

Excellent for ice cream, hot desserts, and peanut butter sandwiches.

RICH CHOCOLATE FROSTING

1/ 2 cup melted butter
2 squares bitter chocolate
1 1/2 cups confectioner's sugar
1 tsp. vanilla
1 egg

Melt butter and chocolate. Add sugar, vanilla, and egg. Beat until smooth.

NOTES

Quick Breads

Pancakes and Doughnuts

" LIGHT, FLUFFY, TENDER, GOLDEN BROWN "

QUICK BREADS

Fluffy Tender Pancakes -- Peach, Blue-
        berry, Banana, Apple, Bacon

Basic Muffin -- Blueberry, Date,
              Fruit, Sunshine

English Muffins

German Coffee Cake -- Lemon Nutmeg
               and Fruit

Corn Bread

Banana Bread

Cranberry Nut Bread

Lemon Bread

Baking Powder Biscuits -- Shortcakes

Swiss Chocolate Doughnuts

Old Fashioned Doughnuts

Raised Doughnuts -- Honey Dipped and
             Jelly

Thrifty Doughnuts

FLUFFY TENDER PANCAKES

2 cups flour
3 3/4 tsp. baking powder
1/2 cup sugar
1/2 tsp. salt
2 eggs
1 1/2 cups water
4 tbs. melted butter

Mix dry ingredients. Beat eggs and water. Add and mix until just blended. Do not overmix. Add melted shortening and blend. Drop on greased griddle. Turn when bubbles appear on one side.

This makes a slightly thick pancake. I use water because it makes a moist tender pancake. If you want richness and more caky, use milk.

VARIATIONS: Add 1 cup berries, diced peaches or bananas, diced apple with cinnamon, or a few bacon bits. Fruit pancakes are excellent with Orange Sauce.

BASIC MUFFIN

2 cups flour
4 tsp. baking powder
1 tsp. salt
3 tbs. sugar
1 egg
1 cup milk
3 tbs. melted butter

(Continued)

BASIC MUFFIN -- (Continued)

Mix dry ingredients. Beat milk and egg together and add. Stir just enough to combine ingredients. Stir in melted butter. Secret to good
muffins is not to overmix. Fill greased muffin
tins one-half full and bake at 400° for 15-20 min.

VARIATIONS

Blueberry: Add 1 cup blueberries to finished
             batter

Date: Add 1/2 cup diced dates

Fruit: Add 1/2 cup diced drained fruit

Sunshine: Add 1 tsp. jam on top of muffin
            batter. As they bake, jam sinks to
            bottom for a change of face

ENGLISH MUFFINS

2 cups scalded milk
1/3 cup shortening
1 tsp. salt
1 tbs. sugar
1 pkg. dry yeast
1/4 cup warm water
2 cups flour
2 1/2 - 3 cups more flour
2 beaten egg whites
Cornmeal

(Continued)

Scald milk. Add sugar, salt, shortening. Cool to lukewarm. Add yeast dissolved in 1/4 cup warm water. Stir in 2 cups flour and beat until smooth. Let rise in a warm place until double in bulk.

Add remaining flour and beaten egg whites. Beat and knead for a fine texture. Let rise until double in bulk.

Roll out on surface sprinkled with cornmeal. Roll to 1/2 inch thick and cut with 3-inch cutter. Let rise until light but not double in bulk.

Cook on hot griddle with sprinkled cornmeal for 15 min., turning frequently during cooking to prevent burning.

Wrap or freeze until ready to toast. Makes 2+ dozen.

GERMAN COFFEE CAKE

1 cup sugar
1/2 cup shortening
2 eggs
1 cup sour cream or sour milk
2 tsp. vanilla
2 cups flour
1 tsp. baking powder
1 tsp. baking soda

TOPPING:
1 tsp. cinnamon
1/2 cup chopped nuts
1/3 cup brown sugar

(Continued)

GERMAN COFFEE CAKE -- (Continued)

Cream shortening and sugar. Beat in eggs; add vanilla. Add dry ingredients and sour milk alternately. Beat until smooth.

Bake in large low pan with topping sprinkled on top and swirled through cake with fork, OR bake in angel food cake tin with layers of batter, topping, batter, topping, and swirl with knife. Bake at 350° for 30-35 min. in low pan, or for 45-55 min. or until it springs back and knife or tester comes out clean if using angel cake tin.

VARIATIONS

Lemon Nutmeg: Add 2 tsp. lemon extract and 1 tsp. nutmeg instead of vanilla

Fruit: Add 1/2 cup blueberries, diced apples, or diced pineapple to finished batter.

CORN BREAD

1 cup cornmeal
1 1/3 cups white flour
2 tbs. sugar
3 tsp. baking powder
1 tsp. salt
1 1/3 cups milk
2 eggs
4 tbs. melted butter or shortening

Mix dry ingredients together. Beat eggs and milk. Add dry ingredients and liquid. Beat until smooth. Add melted butter. Pour into greased pan. Bake at 425° for 20-25 min. until golden brown.

BANANA BREAD

1 3/4 cups flour
2 tsp. baking powder
1/4 tsp. baking soda
1/2 tsp. salt
1/3 cup shortening
2/3 cup sugar
2 eggs
1 cup mashed ripe bananas
1/2 cup chopped nuts

Cream shortening and sugar. Add eggs and beat well. Add dry ingredients alternately with bananas. Blend until smooth. Add nuts. Bake in loaf pan at 350° for about 1 hour or tested done with a clean straw.

CRANBERRY NUT BREAD

2 cups flour
1 cup sugar
1 1/2 tsp. baking powder
1/2 tsp. baking soda
1 tsp. salt
1/4 cup shortening
3/4 cup orange juice
Rind of 1 orange
2 eggs
1/2 cup chopped nuts
1 cup cranberries

Combine dry ingredients. Cut in shortening until blended (small pieces.) Beat eggs and juice together. Add and mix. Add rind; beat. Fold in nuts and whole cranberries. Bake in loaf pan at 350° for about 1 hour.

LEMON BREAD

3 tbs. shortening
1 cup sugar
1 1/2 cups flour
2 eggs
1 tsp. baking powder
1/2 tsp. salt
1/2 cup milk
1/2 cup nuts (optional)
Grated rind of 1 lemon

TOPPING

Juice from 1
lemon plus
1/3 cup sugar

Cream shortening and sugar. Add eggs and beat.
Add dry ingredients and milk. Beat until smooth.
Add nuts and rind. Bake in loaf pan at 325° for 1 hr.
When warm, brush several times with sugar and
lemon juice until you use it all. The sweet bread with
the tart lemon crust is delicious. This is a good sweet
bread to accompany fruit or ice cream.

BAKING POWDER BISCUITS

2 cups flour
1 tsp. salt
4 tbs. shortening
4 tsp. baking powder
3/4 cup milk

Mix dry ingredients. Cut in shortening so that
little pieces slightly smaller than peas are left. Mix
in milk and stir just enough to blend together. Place
on floured counter and cut 1/2 to 3/4 inch thick.
Brush with melted butter. Bake in 450° oven 15 min.
or until golden brown and fluffy and just done in center
when flaked apart. Run to get the butter and jam!!!

For a shortcake for dessert biscuit, add 2 tbs.
sugar to dry ingredients.

SWISS CHOCOLATE DOUGHNUTS

    1 cup sugar
    3 eggs
    1 1/3 cups milk
    2 2/3 tbs. melted shortening
    5 cups flour--maybe a little more
    1/2 cup cocoa
    2 tsp. vanilla
    1 1/8 tsp. baking soda + a pinch
    2 1/3 tsp. cream of tartar
    1 tsp. cinna
    2 tsp. salt
    1/2 tsp. ginger

Beat eggs; add sugar and extract and beat until smooth and light lemon in color. Add milk and melted shortening. Combine all dry ingredients and add to liquids, making sure that cocoa is not lumpy. Stir until smooth.

Roll 1/2 inch thick using as little flour as possible. The softer the dough, the lighter the doughnut.

Cut into doughnuts and fry in fat at 375° until golden brown on both sides and will spring back when pressed against edge.

OLD FASHIONED DOUGHNUTS

1 1/2 tsp. lemon extract
2 eggs
1 cup sugar
1 cup milk
1/3 cup melted shortening
* 5 1/3 cups flour (may vary)
2 tbs. baking powder
1/2 tsp. nutmeg
1/2 tsp. ginger
1 tsp. salt

Beat eggs and extract until frothy. Add sugar and beat until light and fluffy. Add milk and melted shortening. Mix all dry ingredients and add to liquids. Stir until well combined.

Roll 1/2 inch thick on floured surface. Cut into doughnuts and fry at 375° until golden brown on both sides.

After frying, drain on brown paper or paper towels. I use egg cartons and the egg dividers hold the doughnuts from lying flat.

Dip in sugar when slightly cooled, or leave plain.

* Flour will vary. The less flour used to handle the dough, the lighter and more tender the doughnut. You may start with 4 cups and add flour as necessary near end.

RAISED DOUGHNUTS

3 tbs. shortening
2 1/2 tbs. sugar
3 1/2 cups flour
1 1/2 tsp. salt
1/4 tsp. mace
1 1/4 cups milk
1 pkg. dry yeast
1 egg
1/4 tsp. lemon extract

Scald milk. Cool to lukewarm. Dissolve yeast in milk. Add egg, extract, sugar, and shortening. Stir in flour and salt until smooth. Set in warm place with light towel over it and let rise for 30 min. or until doubled in bulk.

Poke down and roll on floured surface to 1/4 inch or a little more. Cut with cutter, or circle for jelly doughnuts. Place on floured cookie sheet or table and let rise until just doubled.

Fry in fat at 375° until golden. These being thick take a little more time than a regular dough-nut.

HONEY DIPPED -- 1 1/3 cups confectioner's sugar, 1 tbs. honey, 6 tbs. hot water. Dip while warm. Drain over cookie rack and re-use drip-ping icing. Keep slightly warm.

JELLY DOUGHNUTS -- Slice and fill with jelly.

THE THRIFTY DOUGHNUT

Use Old Fashioned Doughnut recipe with the following changes:

Use vanilla extract in place of lemon

Add 1 tbs. dry instant coffee and 2 tsp. dry coffee creamer to dry ingredients

This gives you a doughnut with coffee and cream already in it so that all you need is a cup of hot water to drink or for dunking your doughnut.

THRIFTY ? ! ?

"GOLDEN BROWN FRENCH TOAST"

"FLUFFY OMELETTES"

EGGS

Fried Eggs

One Eye Jack

Shirred Eggs

Poached Eggs

Eggs Benedict

Boiled Eggs

Coddled Eggs

Scrambled Eggs

Cheese Omelette

Baked Omelette

French Toast

FRIED EGGS

Have fry pan buttered or use bacon fat.
Break eggs open and cook over low heat. Too
hot will make eggs tough and plastic-like.

ONE EYE JACK

Cut circle out of slice of bread. Brown
bread on one side in fry pan and break egg into
circle. Cook until desired taste.

SHIRRED EGGS

Put a little butter in a small baking dish or
ramekin and place in a 400° oven until butter
melts. Break eggs into dish and return to oven
for a few minutes until done.

POACHED EGGS

Have about 2 inches of water in a pan. Place
salt and about 1 tsp. vinegar in water. This
keeps whites together. Bring to boil, drop eggs
into water. Turn heat down so that eggs just
simmer. Cook until done the way you like them.

EGGS BENEDICT

Toast English muffins. Place slice of cooked ham on muffin. Top with a poached egg and cover with Hollandaise Sauce. A rare treat to wake up to!

BOILED EGGS

The secret to a perfect boiled egg is to have the water boiling and the egg at room temperature, at least not just out of the refrigerator. Prick round end of egg with needle to let air escape. Now we are ready.

Place egg in boiling water

    3 min. - very soft
    4 min. - whites just cooked
    5 min. - whites cooked, yolk runny
    6 min. - whites cooked, yolks wet

    Beyond that you're on your own --
    15-20 min. for real hard

When you remove the egg from boiling water place under cold water for a few seconds to stop heat inside from cooking egg too much.

CODDLED EGGS

Place eggs in boiling water. Turn heat off. Leave eggs for 6 min.

SCRAMBLED EGGS

Scrambled eggs will vary by using different methods. Some use water or milk, others use cream. Some whisk with fork, others use egg beater. How you prepare them is up to your taste, but cooking slowly will prevent browning and give more tender results.

6 eggs
1/4 cup milk
1/2 tsp. salt
1/4 tsp. pepper

Beat with whisk or beater. Pour into buttered fry pan and stir until fluffy and just cooked. Overcooking takes away from the delicate taste of the egg. Considering how hard the hen worked, we should take a few minutes to prepare them!

CHEESE OMELETTE

Follow recipe for Scrambled Eggs. As eggs start to cook, lay slices of American cheese on them and fold over.

BAKED OMELETTE

Place Scrambled Egg mixture in buttered casserole dish. Have egg about 1 inch thick. Sprinkle with your choice of ingredients: ham, onions, peppers, cheese, tomatoes, mushrooms, or whatever. Place in a 425° oven for about 15-20 min. until it puffs and is golden brown. Time will vary with amount of eggs used.

For a light and fluffy Baked Omelette, beat yolks separately. Beat whites stiff and fold in with other ingredients.

This makes a great luncheon meal with a salad.

FRENCH TOAST

4 eggs
1 cup milk
Dash of salt
2 tsp. sugar (optional)

Beat all ingredients together. Dip bread on both sides. Grill in butter until golden brown on both sides. Serve plain or dust with confectioner's sugar in sifter.

Beverages

BEVERAGES

Fruit Punch

Eggnog

Party Punch

Iced Tea

Fruit Cooler

Rum Punch

FRUIT PUNCH

1 can frozen lemonade
1 qt. cranberry juice
1 qt. iced tea
2 cups grape juice
1 qt. gingerale

Add sliced oranges and cherries.

EGGNOG

6 eggs
1/3 cup sugar
Dash of salt
3 tsp. vanilla
1 cup brandy (optional)
1/2 tsp. nutmeg
1 qt. milk (part cream for richness)

Beat eggs until frothy; add sugar and rest of ingredients. Blend until smooth. For a lighter Eggnog, beat egg whites separately and fold into the mixture.

PARTY PUNCH

For a colorful, simple, but very tasty punch, use the following:

1 pint sherbet
1 qt. gingerale or 7-Up

Just before serving, pour tonic over sherbet and it will blend by itself. Rainbow sherbet or mixing sherbets are yummy. Garnish with cherries or sliced fruit.

ICED TEA

To instant tea or regular tea, add a little lemon·juice and instant orange drink mix; or boil one lemon, one orange cut in pieces, and add tea bags to liquid. Sweeten to taste.

FRUIT COOLER

MIX
1 cup pineapple juice
2 cups orange juice
1/2 cup lemon juice
4 tbs. honey
1 qt. gingerale
1 qt. ice water

RUM PUNCH

1 qt. tea
1 bottle rum
1 bottle champagne
Juice of 6 lemons
Juice of 3 oranges
2 cups sugar

Mix and pour over block of ice. Garnish with lemon and orange slices plus a small bottle of maraschino cherries.

For a lighter punch, add 1 to 2 qts. of club soda or tonic water.

Cooking Tips

**START WITH ONE KILO
BUTTER and . . . .**

HINTS AND TIPS

PEELING ONIONS -- Always breathe through mouth while peeling onions and you will never weep another tear. Try it with a clothespin on your nose if you can't keep it closed.

In peeling onions, slice off both ends. Make a slice mark from end to end. Peel one whole layer off with skin in one operation.

COOKED CARROTS -- Left over cooked carrots or squash can be used to make cookies.

LEFT OVER VEGETABLES-- can be used in pot pies and soups rather than mixed and served as a vegetable.

BUTTERNUT SQUASH -- can be peeled with a regular potato peeler rather than with a knife as you have to do with hard shell squash.

BANANAS -- on the green side are much easier to digest than those which are too ripe.

NOTES

NOTES

NOTES

NOTES

NOTES

NOTES

NOTES